Lead On

Lead On

WHY CHURCHES STALL AND HOW LEADERS GET THEM GOING

By
Wayne Schmidt

wesleyan
publishing
house

Indianapolis, Indiana

CONTENTS

—⚏—

FOREWORD

—⟋ⱳ⟍—

You've been there—alone in your office, tired perhaps, and frustrated, wondering, "Why doesn't God . . . *do* something?" As leaders in local churches, we often invest ourselves deeply in ministry. We preach, counsel, pray, and lead with great tenacity. Then, too often, we're disappointed when God doesn't respond to our efforts in the way we'd hoped. Our ministry results are less spectacular than we'd envisioned. There are more setbacks that we'd ever dreamed. There is progress—but it's slow.

I don't know a pastor who hasn't yearned to be more fruitful in ministry. And I know few who haven't felt disappointed or discouraged when those hoped-for results seemed slow in coming.

The Apostle Peter could have been speaking to you and me when he said, "The Lord is not slow in keeping his promise, as some understand slowness. He is patient . . ." (2 Pet. 3:9). One of the most freeing discoveries that I've made about ministry is that God builds *His* church in *His* time. It's pointless to run ahead of God—and often painful! We're always better off to discover God's schedule and work within it rather than trying to impose ours upon Him.

Joshua, the conquering hero of the Promised Land, learned that lesson early in his career. Every success seemed to be followed by a failure, every opportunity accompanied by conflict. In time, though, we see the divine pattern emerge through Joshua's life. We discover that God accomplishes His work through setbacks as well as through success, that conflict and even failure provide the opportunities for leaders to grow, develop the leaders around them, and ultimately move forward to even greater fruitfulness. Through Joshua's life we see that God is always working, even when He seems to be doing nothing at all.

My friend Wayne Schmidt is a rare Christian leader who understands the difference between patience and idleness and who knows how to use God's apparent down time to good advantage. With astounding honesty he recounts the painful mistakes and joyous discoveries that have formed him into the godly and effective pastor that he is. And Wayne's beneath-the-surface look at Joshua's leadership reveals the surprising mix of patience and boldness that enabled this uncanny leader to do what we have all dreamed of—claiming new territory for the King.

This book is a manual for any church leader who has ever been frustrated by the seemingly slow pace of growth. Let these insights encourage and convict you as you lead God's people—sometimes fast, sometimes slow, always in His time.

BILL HYBELS

INTRODUCTION

—⁓⁓—

I closed the door slowly behind me and leaned against it. "I must be getting old," I thought. "That's the third pastor I've talked to this week who has referred to me as a 'mentor.' That's a descriptor I apply to those older and wiser than I."

These three, and others I've interacted with, have so much in common. They're in their first decade of ministry. They're dreamers. Having entered ministry after several years in college or seminary, they have high hopes about what God will accomplish through them. They're passionate, gifted—and somewhat disappointed. They see glimmers of dreams fulfilled, but it's all happening so slowly, more slowly and painfully than they ever imagined.

They're not alone. Ministers who have been serving local churches and leading movements of God for one, two, three, even four decades express similar surprise and discouragement. These individuals have been faithful in serving to the point of self-sacrifice. Yet they are apologetic about the state of their ministries in spite of their steady progress and spiritual health.

These ministers are joined by lay leaders who've invested their gifts and energy in the church. They've studied and attended seminars, seeing in other places what they are praying God will do in their own churches. But it's happening so slowly. . . .

Why does God choose to move slowly?

This isn't merely a hypothetical question for me. I've experienced these slow-motion times in my own ministry. In fact, that's how my ministry began, and that's where it is as I write these words.

In 1979, I joined founding pastor Dick Wynn in planting Kentwood Community Church. Fresh out of college, I envisioned taking the southeast side of Grand Rapids by storm. That spirit of enthusiasm led us to knock on thousands of doors as we established the church, anticipating that hundreds would join us.

That first year we averaged 79 in attendance. The next year, 122. Then Dick was moved to the national office of Youth for Christ, and at age twenty-four I assumed the ill-fitting role of *senior* pastor. By the third year attendance had inched up to 135. The fourth, we topped 150. We were adding people one or two at a time, a dozen or so a year. Not bad, but hardly what I'd envisioned. We believed that the energy we were expending merited much more. It was happening so slowly. . . .

That changed, literally overnight. We built our first facility, and attendance doubled the week we moved in. It took four years to reach the first 160 people and one week to reach the next 160 people! The "go-go" years had begun. We went from 150 to 1,500 in five years. We had been a church where nearly everyone was under thirty years of age. Suddenly, we were reaching people of all ages. The new facility with its increased visibility gave us a new level of credibility in our community. We went from being unknown to being the "talk of the town."

We built our first facility on that site in 1983, added to it in 1984, and added to it again in 1985. A year later we sold the entire property and relocated. We went from a modest six-acre site to a campus of nearly fifty acres. Our "huge" new facility was soon bursting at the seams, with people lined up outside the worship center doors to attend one of the three Sunday morning services. We eventually tried a fourth Sunday morning service, then moved it to Saturday night instead. We were definitely on the fast track. Now *this* is what I envisioned as "normal" when I entered the ministry!

Yet there were challenges. We were growing larger, but the demands of managing our burgeoning facilities, finances, and programming hindered me from frequently asking the questions "Are we growing healthier? Are we reaching spiritually lost people and raising up believers to their full potential in Christ?" We were nearly overwhelmed by transfer growth as people came from surrounding churches to experience the excitement. That distracted us from our clear evangelistic focus. We discovered that some who we thought had bought into our mission were really just enjoying the momentum. We had lots of spectators, but we wondered whether we were nurturing a spirit of servanthood within them.

Over the next dozen years we added another eight hundred people, but growth in attendance had begun to slow. Eventually it tapered off to a plateau, where it's been for the past few years. We were still working hard and, we think, smart, but we are back to slow motion.

STARTING MINISTRY

In 1996, I wrote the book *Leading When God Is Moving*. Based on the first four chapters of Joshua, it examined a time when God was directing His people to claim new territory. It was all happening so fast—for Joshua, for the leaders, for the people. Dramatic changes and visible miracles were an almost daily experience.

That was the start-up phase for the nation of Israel. It was one of those times when God graced a movement with the momentum needed to bring dramatic change. God-given momentum always carries people beyond their comfort zones into the courage zone. No longer languishing in the "maintenance mode" of the wilderness, they move into enemy territory, claiming the land that is promised to them.

Momentum times call for the investment of energy to achieve *expansion*. Like the liftoff of a rocket, the momentum phase burns a lot of fuel, enabling a ministry to budge from its resting place, climb beyond familiar atmosphere and reach previously unreached heights.

Momentum is both exhilarating and exhausting. I've experienced a few of those seasons over the course of my ministry, and look forward to the possibility of enjoying a few more. Momentum times are important for any movement of God. But there are also marathon seasons in ministry, and these are equally valuable.

SUSTAINING MINISTRY

In Joshua chapter 5, the movement of the Israelites ground to a halt. Their progress eventually continued, but it remains slower for the rest of the book. The people still sought to conquer and populate the land God had promised them. Yet while there was still some movement, it wasn't nearly as dramatic as it had been. Why? Had their faith faded? Had their leaders lost their spiritual edge? Was this slowness purely a result of some failure on the human side of the equation?

I puzzled over these questions until I discovered God's Word to Moses in Exod. 23:29–30. There God clearly states that it was His will that the Israelites should take the Promised Land slowly. "I will not drive them out in a single year. . . . Little by little I will drive them out. . . ." Since God intended for them to take the land gradually, that was all He empowered them to do. In this slow-motion mode, they would learn leadership lessons as their movement grew slowly but surely.

During slower growth times, wise leaders invest energy to achieve *excellence*. This is not to say that expansion ceases. But God uses slow-motion times to build strength and depth into the ministry so it not only starts well but also continues strong over the long term. This is the sustainability factor. It is designed to prevent ill-conceived ministry ventures that would never reach fruition. Running a marathon requires perseverance. Slow-growth times are ideal for building sustainability into a ministry.

Tragically, many spiritual leaders squander these slower times in hand-wringing, apologizing, or justifying. They fail to be good stewards by not using these seasons to build the strength needed to sustain a ministry over the long haul. Some things are better done in slow times. During those seasons, one must discover and do the things that can be done best in "such a time as this."

SLOW-MOTION DISCOVERIES

This book, *Lead On,* gleans insights from Joshua's experiences in those "little by little" years. Alongside his biblical journey, I will set some of my own discoveries, made in the context of slower growth. I call them learnings. *Learnings* is an unusual word—one that my wife, who is a language arts teacher, would bring to my attention. This word is meaningful to me because it conveys the idea that learning is an active, ongoing experience that leads to change. It reminds me that within every lesson are the seeds of additional learning opportunities. Here are the learnings I have experienced in times of slower growth.

Learning One: Churches stall when they do not understand God's timing. The greater the difference between God's timetable and mine, the greater the faith and discernment that are required. It is important that every spiritual leader develop an understanding of God's slowness, for "the Lord is not slow in keeping his promise, as some understand slowness" (2 Pet. 3:9). God's patience always has a redemptive purpose, but divine patience must never be confused with human paralysis.

Learning Two: Churches stall when they lose sight of who they are. The first activity of leaders in slow-motion times is to clarify core commitments. That involves renewing passion about the beliefs, values, and actions that honor God, and removing those that dishonor Him. Neither can be done without both vulnerability and vision.

Learning Three: Churches stall when they lose touch with the Source of power. A movement of God draws its fuel from meeting with God. Through prayer we recognize God's power and purpose, thereby positioning ourselves for action. Every step of forward progress involves victory in both physical and spiritual battles.

Learning Four: Churches stall when they fail to build upon God-given victories. There is a spiritual strategy for every victory. Each victory builds momentum as we focus on God, leveraging success into lasting commitment. Leaders must seize opportunities that are disguised as obstacles and reinvest the credibility that victory brings.

Learning Five: Churches stall when they allow themselves to be deceived. Deception is debilitating. Spiritual leaders must never underestimate their capacity to be deceived by Satan, others, or themselves. The downward spiral of deception and disobedience brings disunity and defeat, which stall a movement of God.

Learning Six: Churches stall when leaders do not face their own limitations. It's a pivotal moment when a leader faces personal limitations in the midst of a great mission. While many interpret this moment as the end of their leadership, it is really the beginning of a new way of leading. The multiplication of leaders maintains momentum.

Learning Seven: churches stall when they fail to resolve conflict appropriately. Conflict will cripple a movement of God. Ignoring conflict is not a solution, nor is it consistent with biblical peacemaking. Intentionally addressing conflict honors God and removes a drag from further progress.

Learning Eight: Churches stall when leaders fail to plan for their own transition out of power. A leader's legacy is substantially shaped by the way in which he or she leaves power. The leader's final act must not be a grasp for personal recognition but to help people face the limitations that threaten their full obedience to God. Finishing strong makes a lasting difference.

I'm a hobby runner. One fellow that I run with takes the sport more seriously and has trained extensively. He keeps reminding me that when running longer distances, managing your pace is critical. When you reach a part of the course that is uphill, you must lean into it and pump your arms a bit more to sustain the pace. When running downhill, you should stretch out your legs and relax your arms. After I complete a race, he checks my pulse. Based on my heart rate, he usually delivers the news that I could have done better. My limitations were not physical, but mental; I was capable of more than I thought.

Are you in an uphill time in ministry? Lean into it. Are you enjoying the momentum of a downhill time? Stretch out and make the most of it. My prayer for you is that in each season of your life you will fully utilize your God-given ability. You may be capable of more than you think!

CHAPTER ONE

SLOW

BUT SURE

—~~~—

STALL FACTOR:	Failure to understand God's timing.
FORWARD STEP:	Look for the redemptive purpose behind God's patience.

In January of 2002 leaders from across the denomination in which I serve gathered for the launch of our Leadership Development Journey. Several speakers offered stimulating insights into effective ministry, leaders cast a compelling vision of healthy leaders and churches, and the initial steps of an unfolding adventure were identified. Between the formal sessions there were hundreds of hallway conversations in which we processed what we'd heard and discussed how people in various leadership roles should respond.

A highlight for me was the opportunity to connect with others I see only occasionally and to hear updates on what God is doing in

The reason ninety-nine out of one hundred churches that try to make major transitions fail is that they go too fast.

—Doug Murren

The Lord is not slow in keeping his promise, as some understand slowness. He is patient with you, not wanting anyone to perish but everyone to come to repentance.

—2 Peter 3:9

their lives and ministries. Repeatedly, stories were shared of steady progress in building churches that glorified God. As I listened, I was moved to affirm and celebrate what God was accomplishing through them. But more often than not, before I could speak, I heard a version of these words: "I realize that it's not dramatic, but. . . ." An apology.

That apology is based on what I've come to believe is a misconception: if growth is not explosive, then it is something less than fully honoring to God. That notion is a discredit to the way God often chooses to work. Based on that thinking, we find ourselves offering an apology to others rather than offering glory to God for what He has done.

One of the greatest challenges for believers is to comprehend God's timing. As if discerning the content of God's will is not difficult enough, we must also discern the calendar of His will. I call it the *Timing and Trust Hurdle*. The greater the difference between God's timetable and mine, the greater the faith required. It tests my faith when God moves more quickly than I expect, requiring me to pick up the pace. But the greater test is when God moves more slowly than I expect, requiring me to wait upon Him.

This is not a new challenge for believers and leaders. Understanding God's "slowness" was something the Apostle Peter felt compelled to address just a few years after the resurrection of Christ:

> But do not forget this one thing, dear friends: With the Lord a day is like a thousand years, and a thousand years is like a day. The Lord is not slow in keeping his promise, as some understand slowness. He is patient with you, not wanting anyone to perish, but everyone to come to repentance (2 Peter 3:8–9).

Peter wanted early believers, and us as well, to know that God's perspective on time is not bound by human measurements. He also made clear that we sometimes misread the purpose of God's timing.

God's patience always has a redemptive purpose. His slowness does not indicate a failure to keep His promises. Many of us in church leadership are motivated by God's promises. In addition to the biblical promises that apply to all, we sometimes claim specific promises of ministry fruitfulness. We envision what God has promised to do in reaching the people of our communities and maturing the people of our congregations. When that happens more slowly than expected, we begin to doubt the promises. Instead, we should seek to discover God's redemptive purpose.

As I write these words, I'm searching my own heart. I want to be certain I'm not confusing any leadership paralysis on my part with God's patience. There have been times when I've not moved at the speed God intended. I've been slowed by fear, discouragement, laziness—the list goes on. I never want to misrepresent my tardiness as waiting on God. I've had to repent of the times when God wanted to do more with greater momentum, but I disobediently dragged my feet. Now, every time it seems God has slowed down, I check my own heart, mind, will, and emotions first.

However, I don't want to compound the paralysis by overanalysis! Even the Apostle Paul recognized that some issues of responsibility aren't fully resolved this side of eternity (1 Cor. 4:1–5). Most conscientious church leaders are too hard on themselves and may become crippled by self-recrimination. Once I've searched my own heart, finding forgiveness and learning lessons, I return my focus to the heart of God.

Yes, I have moved slower than God expected. But He has also moved slower than I've expected. If I spend my time waiting upon Him by wringing my hands and wondering why, I squander the opportunity to join Him in the redemptive purpose of His patience. The critical factor in redeeming these slow-motion periods is how I choose to invest the gift of time God has given.

You've heard the maxim "Time heals all things." It's not true. I've seen people use time to become bitter toward God and distant from Him. You've probably seen it too. Time heals only if it is invested in pursuing wholeness over brokenness, forgiveness over bitterness. That is especially true for leaders. Time can be spent asking questions that will likely go unanswered, building frustration in the process. Or it can be invested in building deeper roots, resulting in fruitful ministry. You *can* redeem the time (Eph. 5:15–16).

GOD PROMISES VICTORY, BUT GRADUALLY

The Israelites anticipated entering the Promised Land, and God promised to prepare the way.

> I will send my terror ahead of you and throw into confusion every nation you encounter. I will make your enemies turn their backs and run. . . . I will establish your borders from the Red Sea to the Sea of the Philistines, and from the desert to the River. I will hand over to you the people who live in the land and drive them out before you (Exod. 23:27, 31).

Those promises must have engendered a nervous excitement within the people. They were about to see God work in marvelous ways, but they would be required to do their part. These verses reveal the content of God's will for His people.

Embedded between the two verses quoted above is the calendar of God's will. "But I will not drive them out in a single year, because the land would become desolate and the wild animals too numerous for you. Little by little I will drive them out before you, until you have increased enough to take possession of the land" (Exod. 23:28–29).

This same sense of timing is communicated in Deut. 7:22. While the initial conquest of Canaan would happen quickly, complete victory would be the result of a gradual process. That would allow time for

another of God's promises to be fulfilled. For Moses had also prophe-
sied, "He will love you and bless you and increase your numbers"
(Deut. 7:13). Claiming the promised territory gradually would prevent
the land from returning to a state of natural chaos, as happened later
when Israel was depopulated by the exile of the ten tribes to Assyria (see
2 Kings 17:21–26). The gradual conquest would also serve the purpose
of casting increasing anxiety into enemy nations as they anticipated
their defeat (Exod. 23:27; Deut. 7:23). It is clear that God did not want
the Israelites to misinterpret His timetable, taking His slowness as an
indication that He lacked the power to fulfill His promises.

The book of Judges lists more reasons why Israel was to
inhabit the land gradually. One was that they had violated their
covenant with God after the death of Joshua (Judg. 2:20). Their
failure to listen to God caused Him to say that He would "no
longer drive out before them any of the nations Joshua left when
he died" (Judg. 2:21).

God also sought to test the Israelites' resolve to honor the
covenant and conquer the land (Judg. 2:22–23). This testing would
develop the combat skills of those Israelites who had not fought in
previous wars (Judg. 3:1–2).

Clearly, God had reasons for choosing a slow-motion approach
to leading the Israelites in conquering Canaan. How might those reasons apply to us as we seek to claim new territory for God today?
Let's examine two of them.

He allows us time to grow up + mature

SPIRITUAL FRUITFULNESS: A QUALITY ISSUE

One reason for gradual fulfillment of the promise is identified in
Exod. 23:28. "Because the land would become desolate and the wild
animals too numerous for you." God's aim was to prevent the land
from becoming unfruitful. Quick victory would decrease the quality
of the land. They would acquire much land, but of little worth. It
would be quantity without quality, volume without value.

Sometimes God moves slowly to ensure quality. He wants our

ministries to be spiritually fruitful, not desolate. While we do not fear wild animals, we must never forget that our "enemy the devil prowls around like a roaring lion looking for someone to devour" (1 Pet. 5:8). If we achieve spiritual victories but God doesn't indwell them fully, we become more vulnerable to our enemy than ever before (see especially Luke 11:24–26). Sometimes God works gradually to improve the quality of the result.

As a resident of wintry Michigan, I enjoy the winter sports featured in the Olympic games. I write these words while the winter games of 2002 are taking place in Utah. Downhill skiing is, to me, the most breathtaking event by far. The lone racer dives straight down the mountainside, brushing only a few mandatory gates, building speeds of up to eighty miles per hour. The skiing is exhilarating, the crashes excruciating!

The biathlon is another skiing event, but not nearly so exciting to watch. In this sport, the racer skis cross-country, never achieving great speeds. And he must stop at certain points along the course to shoot at a target. The skier dismounts, aims the rifle, and deliberately slows his heart rate and respiration in order to aim at the tiny target. Compared to downhill skiing, the biathlon is boring! But quality is measured in ways other than raw speed. Accuracy matters too. And in the end, the best athletes in each event receive the same reward—a gold medal.

Does explosive growth always decrease quality? No. Many ministries grow dramatically and stay healthy. Yet a human body that grows dramatically after it has reached maturity is likely to be adding fat, not muscle! It takes time and effort to build muscle. Fat can be added very easily. It can be the same way in ministry.

When I look back at some of the explosive growth in our congregation, I realize that we were adding fat and not muscle. Our body (actually the body of Christ, of which our local church is a part) was growing bigger but not stronger. The people we added were not contributing to the mission but were spectators, observing the increasingly exhausting efforts of those who labored to keep pace with their demands. We developed some of our greatest weaknesses during the go-go years, and some of our greatest strengths in the slow-growth years.

I recently listed some of the ways God's gradual moving has allowed us to strengthen our leaders and our church. Here are a few.

TIME TO MONITOR HEALTH

Slow-growth times have allowed us to monitor the health of our congregation. On an annual basis our church completes the Natural Church Development (NCD) survey.[1] This instrument is designed to measure the characteristics of a healthy church. These are:

- Empowering leadership
- Gift-oriented ministry
- Passionate spirituality
- Functional structures
- Inspiring worship services
- Holistic small groups
- Need-oriented evangelism
- Loving relationships

The key to each characteristic is the modifier. Every church has leadership, but is that leadership empowering others or hindering them? Every church conducts ministries, but are people in those ministries serving according to their gifts or simply filling slots in a program? Each characteristic of church health is measured by its adjective.

While each characteristic is vital for a healthy church, and the goal for every congregation should be increased vitality in each area, it's impossible to improve in all eight areas simultaneously. The evaluation helps by directing attention to the minimum factor—that characteristic that ranks lowest. The NCD survey illustrates the quality characteristics of a church as the staves of a barrel.[2] When the staves of a barrel are of uneven height, the barrel will leak at the top of the lowest stave. Likewise, if the characteristics of a church are of uneven quality, the church's overall health will never rise higher than the lowest characteristic—the minimum factor. Raising the minimum factor allows a church to release a greater share of the potential God has placed within it, and it increases the likelihood of both spiritual and numerical growth.

THE MINIMUM BARREL

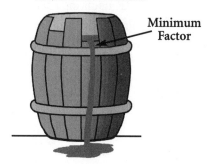

Minimum Factor

The first year we took the survey our minimum factor was functional structures. This factor indicates the clarity of the church's mission, vision, values, and goals. It also reflects the degree to which organizational structures are aligned with the mission, vision, values, and goals. An evaluation of this factor will reveal ways in which a church's leadership either supports or sabotages the fulfillment of the mission, how creative the church is, and how well it manages change.

When the survey revealed that this was our minimum factor, I responded as most pastors do—with denial! How could this be? I had led seminars for other church leaders on vision casting and leadership development! This simply wasn't possible, or so I thought. Yet after overcoming my self-deception and moving beyond the group-think that made us hope only minor adjustments would be necessary, we went to work.

Understand that when a church has just been launched, work in these areas can proceed rapidly. But when a church is more than two decades old and has structures in place that are less than functional (OK, dysfunctional), it's a different story. It took more than a year—and some painful personnel and program changes—to raise this minimum factor.

Attaining health in church life can be a costly and complex process. It takes time, but it's time well spent. God wants His church to be healthy, and while He has little tolerance for time wasting, He graciously allows us to spend time in becoming more vital.

Time for Personal Growth

Slow-growth times also allow for the pursuit of personal and professional growth. That's a daunting challenge for any leader. Tragically, many leaders plateau far too early, putting a lid on their personal development as well as their ministry potential. John Maxwell describes this as The Law of the Lid.

> Leadership ability is the lid that determines a person's level of effectiveness. The lower an individual's ability to lead, the lower the lid of his potential. The higher the leadership, the greater the effectiveness. . . . Your leadership ability—for better or for worse—always determines your effectiveness and the potential impact of your organization.[3]

Maxwell goes on to share the good news that you can raise the lid by increasing your leadership ability.

Some other leaders cease to be effective because they keep moving geographically rather than personally. When their current ministry situation develops to the point where it stretches their ability, they move on to a ministry that allows them to operate within their comfort zone. While there are certainly times when a pastoral change or move to a new church home by a lay leader may be divinely inspired, such changes can be substitutes for the hard work of stretching leadership ability.

I came to Kentwood Community Church in 1979 as a recent college graduate with no full-time ministry experience. The group of six believers that formed the genesis of the church didn't require much leadership! During my first two years in ministry, my mentor and founding pastor, Dick Wynn, stretched me significantly. Then he left, which stretched me even more by placing me in the role of senior pastor. In the two decades since, there have been countless times that my leadership abilities have been tested, found deficient, and forced to expand. Did I immediately see my need to grow and instantly make adjustments? Hardly.

Many of those who serve in important lay leadership roles in our congregation have been with us for most of the church's history. They began in roles that focused more on doing than leading, roles marked more by simplicity than complexity. But over the years new levels of leadership have been required of them, and they've grown to meet the challenges. Those adjustments required the investment of time in learning new skills.

At times every leader has felt like shouting "Wait for me! I'm your leader!" Ideally leaders would always learn new leadership skills before they were necessary. Realistically, we identify the need for those abilities only when circumstances demand them, then work to catch up to those demands. God graciously moves slower at some times to allow leaders to come in step with His plan.

God reveals this never-ending need for growth in leaders in many ways, sometimes through challenging circumstances and at other times through stimulating opportunities. Our church is a satellite location for the Willow Creek Association Leadership Summit, held each August. I remember one year sitting quite contentedly in the opening session of the summit, mentally reviewing the recent strides I'd made as a leader. I'm embarrassed to admit that I was quite full of myself, feeling "on top of my game" as a leader.

Then Bill Hybels began to list the different directions in which leaders need to grow. He talked first of *leading up*, the process of influencing those in authority over us. That's a necessary leadership skill because those in authority can release the resources and exercise the influence that will empower our leadership. I listed some ways I need to relate more effectively to our church board and to my denominational leaders.

Then Bill talked about *leading laterally*, emphasizing the reality that we are all part of a team. Our peers are partners in accomplishing tasks that are beyond our reach as individuals. I have long believed that when God lays before us a great task, He then raises up a great team to complete it. So I made some notes about the teams I'm part of and ways that I could better contribute not only to reaching our goals but also to building up my teammates.

Then he talked about *leading down*, providing what's needed by those who follow us. Since this is the dimension of leadership that I most readily identify with, I reviewed again some areas of growth I'd previously noted. I have the privilege of leading an awesome team of staff and lay ministers, and Bill's comments stimulated some new ideas on how I might become a better servant leader.

Bill concluded by talking about *leading oneself*. He said that the greatest challenge we face is self-leadership. This requires the most significant investment of time and energy. As leaders, we must heighten our capacity for self-awareness, recognizing ways in which we need to grow and change. Then we must deepen our capability for self-discipline so that we will form new habits that will sustain those changes.

When Bill finished his presentation, my previous contentment had been replaced by a new conviction. I realized that the changes I needed to make in each of these directions would take time. My desire was to make steady progress on all fronts. I was humbled by my need to grow as a leader, and these realizations came from only one session—the rest of the conference lay ahead!

We have a God who loves to cause people and leaders to grow. He wants us to be part of what He will do next, not only what He did last. He comes alongside us and—with either a kick to the backside or an arm around the shoulders—moves us forward. It may seem painfully slow at the time, but looking back we can see that we've made progress on the journey.

TIME TO LIVE BALANCED LIVES

God wants us to live balanced lives. God sometimes moves slowly to give us time to grow as leaders, yet He wants us to remain healthy in that process. If all that were required of us was leadership development, perhaps the pace could be picked up. But we are whole people, with physical, emotional, relational, and spiritual needs. We must grow not only as leaders, but as individuals. And as individuals we fulfill roles in families, neighborhoods, communities, and most of all in the body of Christ. That makes life a balancing act.

Our culture celebrates one-dimensional success. We admire the athlete who puts the rest of life on hold in order to reach for the gold. We envy the businessperson who climbs over everyone and everything to ascend the corporate ladder, winning increasingly impressive titles and salaries. We applaud the celebrity who readily sacrifices family on the altar of fame.

I will stand before God someday, but not as a leader only. I will stand as a husband, father, son, and friend. He will assess my stewardship of money, time, and talent. He will also evaluate my management of physical, emotional, and mental health. He'll look inside my soul. On that day, I want to hear "Well done, good and faithful servant" after all those areas are examined.

In late 1984 I made a commitment to live as a whole person. Realizing my inability to accomplish that on my own, I established an accountability partnership with a trusted friend. We have met every other week for the better part of two decades, sharing our dreams and reinforcing our disciplines. Annually we've tweaked our list of accountability goals to help us develop more fully in all dimensions of personal life and in all relationships that we value.

In 1991 I co-authored the book *Accountability: Becoming People of Integrity* to help others learn how to establish accountability partnerships.[4] At that time I expressed the conviction that nothing I had done on a purely human level had done more for my well-being than the establishment of this accountability relationship. That conviction has stood the test of time.

Would it be more efficient to live life one-dimensionally? Yes. Is it more eternally significant to live life multi-dimensionally? Absolutely. There are times when the values of efficiency and eternity collide. Eternal values are always preferable. Life may progress a bit more slowly at those times, but much more fully.

TIME FOR CULTURAL CHANGE

Gradual growth allows time for cultural change, not just circumstantial change. Put another way, it's one thing to modify a program; it's quite another to transform a person. Even more difficult is to transform a church full of people!

Let's suppose that we want to imbed evangelism deeply into our church's culture. There are many training approaches that would be helpful, such as encouraging every member to take a course like *Becoming a Contagious Christian.*[5] Or we might hold special evangelistic events, designed so that members can invite unchurched people from their sphere of influence. We could encourage each member to develop a list of people they love who do not have a personal relationship with Jesus Christ and pray for them regularly.

Would one class, event, or prayer list create a church that has a heart for the lost and prioritize its ministries of outreach? No. It would take repeated seminars, events, and prayer times—as well as modeling by the leaders, testimonies of life change, and messages from the pulpit—to cause an evangelistic heart to beat within the church's culture. It would take repeated emphasis over a period of time.

God sometimes moves slowly so that the things most important to Him will become the things most important to us. Most churches have seen a number of fads come and go. Longtime church members usually develop an initial resistance to any new emphasis, marked by a "this too shall pass" skepticism. Perseverance is the only way to overcome this skepticism. As weeks fade into months, it becomes clear that the new emphasis is not a fad but a significant change in the church's value system.

The Bible is clear about the role of perseverance in the development of an individual's character (Rom. 5:4). Perseverance is also critical to the development of a church's character, or culture. God's patience and our perseverance contribute to producing lasting change. The change must become part of who we are, not just something we do.

I've mentioned just a few areas of church life that may benefit from God's patience. I enjoy watching football on television. One of the things that makes a game interesting is slow-motion replay of important events. After a touchdown catch, for instance, the director will break away from the live action to show a replay of the score in slow motion. It's amazing what you can see in slow motion that you miss at full speed. Slow motion has a way of revealing what really happened so that it becomes obvious which actions were important and need to be maximized and which were futile and need to be discarded.

So it is with slow-motion times in ministry. God may intentionally slow down development so that leaders can see what is really happening and adjust accordingly. He doesn't want us to miss anything, including the qualities that will increase our spiritual effectiveness.

SPIRITUAL FITNESS: A QUANTITY ISSUE

Another reason that God sometimes moves slowly is identified in Exod. 23:29, where Moses stated that God would not allow the Israelites to conquer the land "until [they had] increased enough to possess it." God was concerned about their capacity to populate the Promised Land. Overall population was not the issue. God's plan called for each tribe of Israel to take responsibility for inhabiting a certain section of the land.

Sometimes God moves slowly to allow us to acquire the necessary spiritual fitness to fully possess His promises. It's a capacity issue.

The most common measurement of quantity in the church is attendance. When we think of capacity, we may think of the seating capacity of the church building. Those are visual, and sometimes helpful, quantitative measurements. But there are other issues that relate to quantity in the church.

LEADERSHIP QUANTITY

For a ministry to move forward, the quantity of its leaders must increase. Different ministries, by their very nature, require different numbers of leaders. In some public meeting rooms it's required that the legal capacity of the room be posted. I wonder if it would be helpful for some ministries to post their necessary leadership capacity. The way we overload some leaders ought to be illegal!

During periods in our church's history when attendance was increasing rapidly, it was quite easy to keep up with the challenge of increasing worship leadership capacity. We could add hundreds in attendance by simply adding a service. Since each service was a duplicate of the others, we simply asked the existing leaders to come an hour early or stay an hour later. We added hundreds of attendees—but few new leaders.

Consider, however, what it would be like to add even one hundred attendees to a small group ministry. Ideally, you would have a group leader for every ten people or so. Each of those leaders would have an apprentice. Since it's helpful to have a coach for every five leaders, you'd also need to add a couple of coaches. So adding one hundred people in attendance at small groups might require the identification of at least twenty new leaders, and that doesn't include those who serve in other leadership roles within a group!

That's why small group multiplication requires a greater investment of time and resources than does the addition of worship attendees. When growing rapidly, it is hard to keep up the leadership capacity for small groups. Looking back, I realize that our worship attendance outstripped our small group formation. The result was that we had more "spectators" in our services, who were only loosely connected to the community of the church. The church seemed more impersonal during that period, and since life change usually happens best in small groups, there was less forward progress spiritually.

Many churches try to resolve the capacity issue by adding to the load of existing leaders. In some ministries this is workable, but not in most. Our children's pastor has discovered that the multiplication of leaders is key to retaining existing leaders because placing a greater load on existing leaders increases burnout. When a person is burned out in a ministry, he or she tends to warn others of the danger, causing potential leaders to avoid volunteering in that area. In fact, our children's pastor has found that it's easier to fill twenty positions that have a reasonable load limit than it is to fill ten positions that are on overload.

So God may cause growth to happen more slowly to allow the leaders to emerge who will adequately staff the ministries required for a healthy church. In the wonderful leadership book *Good to Great*, author Jim Collins comments on increasing leadership capacity in a chapter entitled "First Who . . . Then What." Jim points out a problem that plagues not only corporations but also congregations. That is defining the "What" of the organization—the mission, vision, and strategies—without defining the "Who"—the people who are necessary to reach the goal. Without people, the mission is merely words on paper. Jim makes the point using the analogy of a bus. "If we get the right people on the bus, the right people in the right seats, and the wrong people off the bus, then we'll figure out how to take it to someplace great."[6]

I have used that image as a guideline for my private leadership prayers:

- *The right people on the bus.* "O Lord, please draw by Your Spirit those people you want to function as part of Your Body in our local church."

- *The right people in the right seats.* "Help us to prepare them for works of service by identifying their passions, gifts, and personality, matching that to the ministry in which they will experience the greatest fulfillment and fruitfulness."

- *The wrong people off the bus.* "Lord, protect us from unfruitful, critical people. As the Gardener (Luke 15), do Your work of removing or pruning. Amen."

If God wants to take us someplace great, He'll raise the right leaders to get us there and remove those who aren't contributing. But this raising and removing takes time.

OWNERSHIP CAPACITY

A second aspect of quantity is ownership capacity. Slow motion allows time for slower adopters to get on board with needed changes, creating the momentum needed to proceed.

It's amazing the methods God sometimes uses to give the insight necessary for making life change. One day I was having breakfast in a fine dining establishment near my home, Mr. Burger (yes, the name says it all). Since it's a good place to get a reasonably priced breakfast, I'm not the only pastor who frequents it. In keeping with the nature of the fine dining experience that Mr. Burger strives to create, there are no waiters. Diners file through a line to order breakfast, pay for it at the end of the counter, then wait for their number to be announced over the loud speaker. Sometimes the line backs up a bit.

Enough about the restaurant. As I was standing in line, I struck up a conversation with a pastor whose church had recently completed a building program. The program was controversial because it required the demolition of the original church building in order to erect the new one in its place. Several longtime members had vocalized their opposition, some of which was accompanied by threats to leave or withhold funds if the plan proceeded. In spite of this, the expansion was approved by a congregational vote and the necessary pledges were received.

This pastor, about twenty years older than I and considerably wiser, shared with me some of his experiences as a leader during that event. I asked if the opposition group remained in the church. He said some had left, but those who remained had come to appreciate the new addition and were returning to a more supportive stance toward the church. He went on to say that they were in the process of furnishing the facility, and he was asking those who had not contributed to the building itself to contribute to the furnishings.

It was the reason he gave for this that captured my attention. For it was not that the project really needed additional financial support—it had come in well within budget. However, the pastor related

Grace

that in their initial opposition, these people had gone way out on a limb with their harsh comments. Now, he said, "I'm trying to give them some time to come in off the limb."

His remarks were filled with grace. Many leaders would advocate "cutting off the limb" and letting them fall because of their opposition. But grace and time were giving the late adopters an opportunity to be part of what God was doing.

In my first book based on Joshua, I recognized the work of Aubrey Malphurs and others who identified differing rates at which church members adopt new ideas.[7] Some people are initially responsive to change, while others are initially resistant to it. While it's true that you can't wait for everybody—even God won't do that—additional time may allow more people to invest themselves in the new thing God is doing. God sometimes moves slowly in order to increase ownership capacity of a ministry.

REBALANCING

The third way that slow motion affects quantity is that it allows time to rebalance uneven growth. Churches tend to grow unevenly, and perhaps leaders do as well. We don't develop our abilities simultaneously or equally. We make strides in one area, which leaves us scrambling to catch up in others. This phenomenon results from what's often called the Principle of Uneven Development.

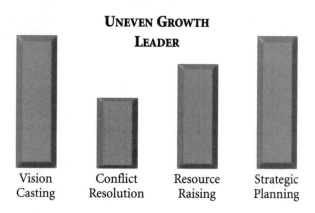

UNEVEN GROWTH
LEADER

Vision Casting • Conflict Resolution • Resource Raising • Strategic Planning

CHURCH DEPARTMENTS

| Worship and Creative Parts | Children | Youth | Adults |

Uneven development is seen most tangibly in the development of church facilities. Back in 1997 we completed our new sanctuary, which we call our Celebration Center. While most of our facilities have been built a piece at a time, an auditorium is very difficult to build in pieces! So we took a big step of faith and built a sanctuary we believed would serve both our immediate and ultimate needs. It is a wonderful facility. It allowed us to retain our single Saturday evening service and return to two services on Sunday morning (as opposed to three or four).

However, if the auditorium were filled to capacity in our weekend services, it would be impossible for us to provide the necessary space for children's and youth ministries. We knew that when we built the auditorium, but we also knew that we didn't have the resources to provide all the space we would eventually need at once. We added the Ground Zero Student Center four years later, but have yet to add adequate children's space or the adult classroom space needed to accommodate a capacity crowd. The years that have passed since the Celebration Center was completed are allowing us to begin rebalancing our facilities.

Ministries usually develop in that unbalanced way also, since it is very difficult to advance all types of ministry simultaneously. A church may emphasize children's ministry for a while, resulting in an influx of young families to the church. Before long, marriage and family classes will need to be added to the adult curriculum, along with small groups for younger couples and youth ministries for older siblings. About the time those ministries are in place, the children's ministry will need attention again!

Rebalancing takes time. If some capacities are underdeveloped, and if that uneven development is exaggerated by explosive growth, the church may become unhealthy. God's patience allows for the rebalance.

Not far from where I live there is a dynamic new church. Since its founding pastor, Jim Miller, came to town, I've met with him on a monthly basis. The initial stages of this church's development grew painfully slow. Like most high-powered leaders, Jim was chomping at the bit. In those early days, he shared with me more stories about frustration than fruit. Why was everything taking so long? Jim used his abundant energy not only to lead services at his new church but also to commute a few miles to speak at a nearby church that was struggling.

Little did he know that in God's timing the members of the struggling church would unanimously vote to close their doors and *give* their building to the fledgling congregation. The fine, ideally-located facility combined with the new church's energy created tremendous momentum for reaching this community for Christ! Was the slow motion of the early days a result of God's orchestrating two churches at different life stages to converge and do something great? I'd say yes!

We may not always know why God chooses to give victory gradually. I've come to accept that some of the reasons will remain a mystery. But many of them can be identified and ought to be celebrated. Let us never make excuses or apologize to one another for those times when God moves slower than expected. Instead, let's give Him glory and get on with His business.

PERSONAL REFLECTION

1. Is there an area in your personal life where you are disappointed that God hasn't done more or moved faster?

2. An examination by a medical doctor assesses physical health.

Take a moment for a personal examination of your spiritual health.

> *Diagnosis*—Is there any problem in your spiritual health? If so, what?

> *Prescription*—In what might you improve your overall spiritual health?

3. Is your life now in balance? What areas are receiving too much of your energy and attention? What areas are being neglected?

4. Apply the Principle of Uneven Development to your personal life. In what areas have you grown rapidly? In what areas might you need to do some catching up?

Inventory for Spiritual Leaders

1. Why do you think many pastors and lay leaders apologize for slow growth?

2. Name some ways in which slower growth may allow for quantitative developments (though not guarantee it).

3. How would you rate the current health of your church or the ministry area you lead? Why?

4. In what areas is God currently asking you to grow as a leader?

5. Which dimension of leadership do you find most difficult? The easiest?

    ___ Leading Up

    ___ Leading Laterally

    ___ Leading Down

    ___ Leading Yourself

6. In what areas of ministry do you currently need more leaders?

7. What areas of your ministry need to be rebalanced?

Joshua's Journal

Lord, your ways are far beyond me. I don't understand them. I feel the challenge of knowing *what* You are going to do. That challenge is amplified by trying to discern *when* You are going to do it. Help me to discover all that You choose to reveal to me. But help me also to keep growing and learning at those times when I don't understand. Don't allow the mystery of Your will to stall my commitment to the ministry You want to accomplish through me. Amen.

CLARIFYING
CORE COMMITMENTS

—◊◊◊—

> **STALL FACTOR:** Loss of focus.
> **FORWARD STEP:** Renew your allegiance to God.

If I'd been leading the Israelites, my reaction would have been "You've got to be kidding me. This is neither the time nor the place."

The fourth chapter of Joshua ends with the miraculous crossing of the Jordan River by the Israelites. That dramatic transition resulted in Joshua being exalted and revered in all of Israel (4:14) and the peoples of the land knowing that the Lord is powerful (4:24).

So what happened next? Any leader would have sought to capture the momentum generated by the miraculous crossing to motivate his troops for battle. That momentum had already weakened the enemies' defenses—"their hearts melted and they no longer had the courage to

With the power of conviction, there is no sacrifice.

—Pat Benatar

For we know, brothers, loved by God, that he has chosen you, because our gospel came to you not simply with words, but also with power, with the Holy Spirit and with deep conviction

—1 Thessalonians 1:4–5

face the Israelites" (5:1). It was the perfect situation for quick action.

"At that time the LORD said to Joshua. . . ." (5:2). What? "Go get 'em!"? "Strike while the iron is hot!"? No, God decided that the time was right for the men of Israel to be circumcised. *Circumcised!* As I said, my reaction would have been "You've got to be kidding!"

Crossing the Jordan had removed the last natural barrier between Israel and her enemies. They were officially in enemy territory, therefore vulnerable to attack. If circumcision was necessary, it should have been done on the other side of the river. All the men of Israel would have known about the short-term debilitating effects of circumcision. Their oral traditions would have included the account of the Shechemites, who were tricked into being circumcised and then slaughtered and looted while they were still in the painful phase of recovery (Gen. 34).

Why would God leave His people vulnerable just as they set foot in the Promised Land? Why would He slow them down when acting with speed seemed likely to bring victory?

I'm slowly catching on to the fact that if God's action doesn't make sense to me, that doesn't mean it's a mistake. Usually, it means there's a lesson for me to learn. Often it's the same lesson He wanted Joshua and the people of Israel to learn before their battles began.

Earlier, God had promised victory, but "little by little." The promise of victory in Exodus, chapter 23, is bracketed by commands to worship God alone. God introduces His promise with these words: "Do not bow down before their gods or worship them or follow their practices. You must demolish them and break their sacred stones to pieces. Worship the LORD your God . . ." (Exod. 23:24–25a).

God concluded His promise by repeating that admonition: "Do not make a covenant with them or with their gods. Do not let them live in your land, or they will cause you to sin against me, because the worship of their gods will certainly be a snare to you" (Exod. 23:32–33).

Stated negatively, God's command prohibits expressions of allegiance to other gods. Stated positively, the people are called to worship God and look to Him alone for blessings.

There could be no more tangible, personal expression of allegiance to the God of Israel than circumcision. More than a physical act or medical procedure, it was a spiritual act that would position them to be empowered by God to conquer the Promised Land. To undergo circumcision would be a clear sign of their obedience to God.

A SIGN OF REPENTANCE

Joshua 5:4–7 gives the background on why this generation of Israelites had not been circumcised:

> All those who came out of Egypt—all the men of military age—died on the way after leaving Egypt. All the people that came out had been circumcised, but all the people born in the desert during the journey from Egypt had not. The Israelites had moved about in the desert forty years until all the men who were of military age when they left Egypt had died, since they had not obeyed the LORD. For the LORD had sworn to them that they would not see the land that he had solemnly promised their fathers to give us, a land flowing with milk and honey. So he raised up their sons in their place, and these were the ones Joshua circumcised. They were still uncircumcised because they had not been circumcised on the way.

The circumcision of this generation marked the close of a dark chapter in the history of Israel, one marked by faithlessness and wandering.

The previous generation, which had refused to follow God's lead, had died off. The generation that had been born in the desert had entered the Promised Land. But the men of this generation had never been circumcised. Now the one thing needed to place them in right standing with God was being accomplished. They were no longer uncircumcised wanderers born of disobedient parents, but circumcised conquerors. This event was their opportunity to establish a new pattern of obedience in their own generation.

The only way to leave behind a sinful past is to repent. God may slow us down to indicate that something needs to be removed from our lives before we can fully embrace His plan for the future. In order to repent, we must overcome the human tendencies toward denial, blame, and rationalization. We'd like to believe that we always respond immediately to God's conviction, but often we don't repent until He has repeatedly revealed the need for change. Once we do come to grips with His revelation, we must take responsibility before God for our sins of commission and omission.

The church I grew up in had an informal approach to worship, so I learned little about the seasons of the church year that are observed by the liturgical churches. Yes, we celebrated Christmas and Easter, but we didn't formally recognize that Christmas is part of the season of Advent or that Easter is the culmination of the Lent. This was true also of Kentwood Community Church for many years after its founding. Over time, however, we've added some observance of those seasons to our worship. We now use Advent candles and special readings on the Sundays leading up to Christmas. We also observe the Lenten season by the imposition of ashes on Ash Wednesday, by receiving communion on Maundy Thursday, and by symbolizing the Cross on Good Friday and the empty tomb on Easter Sunday.

Ash Wednesday has become one of the most significant services in our annual calendar. Perhaps that's because repentance is so seldom emphasized in today's celebrative worship climate. This day seems to tap our longing for some tangible way of showing humility—how else does one demonstrate humility in a public setting without appearing prideful?

The Ash Wednesday service of 2001 marked the close of a difficult chapter in the life of our church. I stood before the congregation as their spiritual leader and confessed the ways in which I had limited the freedom of God's Spirit to work among us. Some of my confessions were things I had done; others were matters I'd left undone. As I looked into the faces of those who felt the impact of my sin and shortcoming, God broke my heart and tears began to flow. His Spirit produced godly sorrow as I read these words: "I, Wayne Schmidt, as senior pastor and team leader for the spiritual health of Kentwood Community Church, have felt led by the Spirit of God to repent of the following sin." One by one I named them:

- Being distracted from my primary calling to provide spiritual leadership.
- Allowing my heart for spiritually lost people to cool, downplaying the reality that hell is a real place and that real people go there.
- Avoiding conflict, allowing tensions and dissension to take root.
- Not praying with the faith and fervency that marked my prayers in the early days of Kentwood Community Church.
- Lacking boldness to declare the "truth in love," at times settling for what pleased people rather than what pleased God.

While these sins may not sound as dramatic as moral failure or criminal behavior, they were wrong in God's sight nonetheless. I was careful to avoid grandiose statements that would make the situation sound scandalous while I frankly admitted that my shortcomings had hindered God's work among us. This confession did not lead to a forced resignation but to a new direction.

Following my statement, representatives from our staff and church board led the congregation in a litany of confession. Some of the shortcomings mentioned in the litany had been downplayed or denied for years. Now they were written out by our leadership team and spoken out by our church family. We sensed that God was honored by our specific, corporate confession. Here is some of what we recited together:

> We have not persevered in developing important spiritual initiatives in evangelism, serving, and fellowship. Instead, we have continually started new programs rather than fully integrating initiatives into the culture of Kentwood Community Church. This lack of perseverance has caused us to keep trying new things while leaving critical areas of church health to die a slow death. We have missed the character development and joy that comes with perseverance.

> Our unwillingness to deal with differences and conflict has led to a proliferation of gossip and slander, resulting in division between us. This critical spirit has affected both our fellowship as believers and the witness of the church, dishonoring our Lord Jesus who prayed that we might be one in order that the world may know Him.

> We have approached worship with a "what's in it for me" mind-set rather than asking "what can I offer to God?" Our preferences have become central, rather than the desire to give You praise. This has made us, mere creatures, the center of attention, rather than our God who is forever to be praised.

Then we used ashes to make the sign of the Cross on the forehead of each person who wished to display that mark of personal repentance and humility. Sorrow turned to joy as hundreds of people tangibly indicated their desire that the future be different than the past.

As a congregation, this was our *act* of repentance, a display of godly sorrow. We could identify with the Corinthians when Paul wrote, "Godly sorrow brings repentance that leads to salvation and leaves no regret, but worldly sorrow brings death" (2 Cor. 7:10). During the remaining Wednesdays of the Lenten season we met and prayed that we might display the *fruit* of repentance. Paul wrote, "See what this godly sorrow has produced in you: what earnestness, what eagerness to clear yourselves, what indignation, what alarm, what longing, what concern, what readiness to see justice done. At every point you have proved yourselves to be innocent in this matter" (2 Cor. 7:11). We devoted those prayer meetings to asking God to empower us in each area we'd confessed so that we might "prove our repentance by our deeds" (Acts 26:20).

Would we have reached that point of repentance as a congregation if we were moving at full speed? While I'd like to think we would have, I believe that the atmosphere most conducive to reflection and confession rarely occurs in a time of momentum. This is not to say that our example is the ideal. In some ways, it's embarrassing to admit that God had to slow us down to a near stop before we acknowledged our sins and shortcomings. It is entirely possible to build in periodic times of reflection, including confession and correction if necessary, so that unconfessed sin does not hinder steady forward progress. That is true both for individuals and for congregations.

In the book *Working with Emotional Intelligence,* the author outlines five characteristics of people who are effective in the marketplace.[1] The first two are integrally linked to repentance. The first is *self-realization,* having a conscious awareness of your attitudes and actions so that you know your strengths and weaknesses. The second is *self-discipline,* having the ability to form new habits. Leaders and congregations both need to take time to realize what needs to change and to discipline themselves to make those changes.

Immediately after the men of Israel were circumcised, the Lord said to Joshua, "Today I have rolled away the reproach of Egypt from you" (5:9). Commentators differ on the exact meaning of this pronouncement. Some believe it is a reference to the fact they had entered the Promised Land, successfully completing their journey from Egypt. Yet since it immediately follows the circumcision, others believe it means that they had finally separated themselves from the last vestige of Egyptian bondage. Whatever its exact meaning, it's clear that God's people had rewritten an old script. They had closed an old chapter of disobedience and opened a new chapter of obedience. They dealt with the past so they could move unhindered into the future.

A SIGN OF RELIANCE

What makes a leader or a group of people more reliant upon God? If dependence upon God increases effectiveness for God, what kind of environment fosters the greatest level of trust? I'm currently in the process of memorizing passages from John, chapter 15, where Jesus described for His disciples that level of dependence that is required for spiritual fruitfulness. Jesus said:

> Remain in me, and I will remain in you. No branch can bear fruit by itself; it must remain in the vine. Neither can you bear fruit unless you remain in me. I am the vine; you are the branches. If a man remains in me and I in him, he will bear much fruit; apart from me you can do nothing. . . . If you remain in me and my words remain in you, ask whatever you wish, and it will be given you (John 15:4–5, 7)

As followers of Christ, we are to rely upon Him for the ability to be effective as a branch relies upon the vine to provide the nutrients it needs to bear fruit.

The ideal condition for creating greater reliance upon God occurs when we simultaneously sense our powerlessness and His powerfulness. That condition is represented by this formula:

Our Powerlessness x God's Power = A New Level of Reliance

That's exactly where the Israelites found themselves. They had just crossed the Jordan River, aided by God's miraculous intervention. Joshua then told the people why God performed the miracle and why they were to memorialize the moment:

> For the LORD your God dried up the Jordan before you until
> you had crossed over. The LORD your God did to the Jordan
> just what he had done to the Red Sea when he dried it up
> before us until we had crossed over. He did this so that all the
> people of the earth might know that the hand of the LORD is
> *powerful* and so that you might always fear the LORD your
> God (Josh. 4:23–24, emphasis mine).

That's one half of the equation—the evidence of God's power.

What about the other half—their sense of powerlessness? That's exactly what the circumcision would create. Their fighting men would be incapacitated, leaving them completely vulnerable except for the protection of God "as they remained where they were in the camp until they were completely healed" (5:8).

I'm convinced this is the reason God waited until they had entered the Promised Land to command the Israelites to be circumcised. After any powerful movement of God, human beings are inclined to think we can build upon it. We feel personally powerful because we've been in a situation where God has shown Himself powerful. So God often chooses those moments to put us in a place where we sense our vulnerability.

One of the greatest challenges of spiritual leadership is the stewardship of power. We usually think of stewardship as managing hard assets—measurable things like money and time. But leaders must manage soft assets as well—things like credibility, spiritual gifts, influence, and yes, power. We become better stewards of power as we recognize that all of it belongs to God and that He can exercise it through the life of any devoted person. He sovereignly chooses to do His work through us, and we are blessed simply to be present when His power is manifested.

We are partnering with other churches in our region to reach our community for Christ. Certainly we must do our part in directly influencing spiritually lost people through the ministries of our congregation. Yet we recognize that new churches are often more effective in reaching spiritually lost people. So we're partnering with other congregations to plant churches. Why are new churches usually more effective in doing evangelism than existing churches? There are a lot of reasons—they're not bound by tradition, they don't have as many "power blocks" within the church, they aren't as focused on meeting the needs of existing members, and the list goes on. I would add this item—they are more likely to rely on God's power instead of their own resources.

When a new church begins, its human resources are extremely limited. Church planters have a big vision and an empty bank account. If God doesn't show up, they won't survive, let alone thrive. But as churches age, they gain resources—members, facilities, programs. They develop the ability to survive for many years whether God shows up or not! We all know of churches that are spiritually dead, entirely void of God's Spirit, and yet meet every week.

Reflect on your own church's history. You may discover that the most fruitful times were when you took the risk of going beyond your own resources to rely upon God. When we relocated to our current property, not one financial institution was willing to provide the resources that our young church needed. We went out on a limb, accepting a God-sized challenge that stretched every person in our congregation. We all knew that if God didn't show up, there would be no backup plan. We were completely dependent upon Him.

Now we're entering another building program. For more than twenty years we've operated with financial integrity. Several banks are competing to provide financing, even encouraging us to borrow more than we'd like. We could borrow the amount needed to supplement a comfortable level of giving without relying upon God's power. Is that a good place to be? No! It is a very dangerous place to be.

Risk yields reward, and that's especially true when relying upon God. Imagine two circles, one within the other.

If we live and exercise leadership within the circle of our own power, we will be comfortable. We'll always be able to do what we choose to do even if God does nothing. But our circle of influence, the difference we can make in the world, will be limited. We're a big fish in a small pond, the pond of our own power. When we reach beyond what we can accomplish with our own thinking and doing, we take the risk of radical reliance. We enter the realm of God's power. Less comfortable? Absolutely! Yet will that act of courage make us candidates to witness a movement of God? Undoubtedly.

Tragically, as churches and leaders mature, they operate more and more within the realm of their own power and less and less within the realm of God's power. The average church plateaus in growth before it is twenty years of age. When does the average spiritual leader plateau in personal growth and effectiveness? By thirty years of age? Forty? A leader's personal power expands as he or she develops new resources—the inner circle grows. But a little more of our power is a sorry substitute for a little more of God's power, which is available only when we take the risk of abandoning our resources to rely on God.

Warning! The risks we take must be acts of faith, not foolishness. They must result from obedience to God's leading. The men of Israel were vulnerable because they obeyed God's command to be circumcised, not because of some rash decision. Vulnerability, by itself, has no value. Reliance that honors God is always a byproduct of obedience.

This issue becomes more complex for us as leaders when we realize that the method of reliance is just as important as the level of reliance. *How much* we rely upon God is not the only issue. *How* we rely on Him matters as well. Relying upon God in the future will not require simply "more of the same." In the desert, the Israelites relied upon God for food by eating His daily provision of manna. In the Promised Land, God moved them beyond a manna mentality.

> On the evening of the fourteenth day of the month, while camped at Gilgal on the plains of Jericho, the Israelites celebrated the Passover. The day after the Passover, that very day, they ate some of the produce of the land: unleavened bread and roasted grain. The manna stopped the day after they ate this food from the land; there was no longer any manna for the Israelites, but that year they ate of the produce of Canaan (Josh. 5:10–12).

From now on, Israel would not simply collect food. Now they must conquer in order to eat. They would have to rely on God both at new levels and in new ways. That's the essence of spiritual growth and leadership development.

A SIGN OF RENEWAL

Circumcision was instituted as the sign of God's covenant with the nation of Israel.

> Then God said to Abraham, "As for you, you must keep my covenant, you and your descendants after you for generations to come. This is my covenant with you and your descendants after you, the covenant you are to keep: Every male among you shall be circumcised. You are to undergo circumcision, and it will be a sign of the covenant between me and you" (Gen. 17:9–11).

By being circumcised, descendants of Abraham indicated their commitment to keep their part of the bargain. God's faithfulness in the covenant is never at issue—He always keeps His word. The question mark is on the human side of the agreement. God looks for our commitment to His work not because He needs us but because He has soverignly chosen to work through us. That notion is aptly expressed in the saying "Without God, we can not. Without us, He will not."

Circumcision slowed the pace for Israel. The healing process required them to "camp until they were healed." While camping, they celebrated the Passover. They had shed their own blood to demonstrate their commitment to covenant keeping. Then they celebrated the Passover, shedding the blood of a lamb as a reminder of God's part in covenant keeping.

God still requires circumcision as a sign of our willingness to keep His covenant. But there is a new covenant in force.

> "The time is coming," declares the LORD, "when I will make a new covenant with the house of Israel and with the house of Judah. It will not be like the covenant I made with their forefathers when I took them by the hand to lead them out of Egypt, because they broke my covenant, though I was a husband to them," declares the LORD. "This is the covenant I will make with the house of Israel after that time," declares the LORD. "I will put my law in their minds and write it on their hearts. I will be their God, and they will be my people" (Jer. 31:31–33).

This new covenant, accomplished by the shedding of the blood of Jesus Christ, is what we remember through communion (Mark 14:24). It's the covenant mediated by Christ (Heb. 9:15).

And this new covenant is signified by a new circumcision. It is a circumcision of the heart.

> A man is not a Jew if he is only one outwardly, nor is circumcision merely outward and physical. No, a man is a Jew

if he is one inwardly; and circumcision is circumcision of the heart, by the Spirit, not by the written code. Such a man's praise is not from men, but from God (Rom. 2:29).

Circumcision of the heart also involves wounding and healing. The act of circumcision may slow our pace so we can experience the change of heart that God requires.

For Israel, the covenant was the framework for what they believed and how they behaved. It was vital that they renew that covenant before they undertook a task as great as the conquest of Canaan. As leaders and as churches, it is important that we periodically renew our commitment to the beliefs and behaviors that attend our covenant with God.

BELIEFS

It's unfortunate that most Christians exhibit little desire to understand what they believe. Perhaps overreacting to the days when Christians were divided by petty differences, Christians today are all too quick to dismiss any discussion of doctrine as divisive. Their mantra is "It doesn't really matter what we believe as long as we love Jesus." I support the desire to love Christ with greater intensity, but I also advocate the need to believe in Him with greater clarity.

The church I serve holds doctrinal positions that are mostly in common with other evangelical churches. Our distinctive doctrine, however, differs from the dominant Christian belief system in our community. In membership classes we seek to clearly explain our beliefs. I see many people in those classes who, without a moment's hesitancy, set aside beliefs they've held for decades in order to embrace ours. And I'm not naïve—if they change churches again, they will likely set aside our beliefs to embrace those of yet another church. Doctrines are no longer anchor points for faith, but words on paper subject to regular revision.

At Kentwood Community Church, we believe that "fully committed believers live belief-based, value-centered, mission-motivated lives." We encourage members to examine our beliefs carefully and consider what they personally believe. To prompt that reflection, we have added a reflective component to each of our doctrinal statements. Here's an example, taken from our statement on "God's Word, the Bible."

We believe that the books of the Old and New Testaments constitute the Holy Scriptures. They are the inspired and infallibly written Word of God, fully inerrant in their original manuscripts and superior to all human authority, and have been transmitted to the present without corruption of any essential doctrine. We believe that they contain all things necessary to salvation; so that whatever is not read therein, nor may be proved thereby, is not to be required of any man or woman that it should be believed as an article of faith, or be thought requisite or necessary to salvation. Both in the Old and New Testaments life is offered ultimately through Christ, who is the only Mediator between God and humanity. The New Testament teaches Christians how to fulfill the moral principles of the Old Testament, calling for loving obedience to God made possible by the indwelling presence of His Holy Spirit.

Do you believe what our church believes?

_____ I believe the Bible is God's inspired Word and is fully authoritative in determining the way I should live my life.

_____ I believe God's Word is to be trusted more than my own thoughts, experiences, and feelings when determining what is best for me.

_____ I believe human teaching is to be tested by its compatibility with God's Word.

By adding an opportunity for response to each of our eleven belief areas, we're helping people to internalize their beliefs.

BEHAVIORS

Our behaviors are the tangible expression of our values. Years ago I was challenged by a speaker who asserted, "What you value has absolutely nothing to do with what you say." After a pregnant pause, he went on to say, "What you value has absolutely everything to do with what you do." The rest of his unsettling presentation exposed our regrettable tendency to measure spiritual development by "talking the talk" rather than "walking the walk." It's much easier to improve our vocabulary than to systematically incarnate our values in everyday life.

Our need for repentance as a church, and my need as a leader, rose partly from the incongruity that had developed between our stated values and our characteristic actions. Part of the fruit of our repentance was that we spelled out our conviction that "fully committed believers live belief-based, value-centered, mission-motivated lives" by listing the specific values that we hope to exhibit. We ended up with eleven:

- Accountability.
- Awareness of and biblical approach to cultural issues.
- Biblical communication.
- Fellowship.
- Growing relationship with Jesus Christ demonstrated by life change.
- Loving one another.
- Prayer.
- Reaching out to spiritually lost people.
- Servanthood through gift-based ministry.
- Stewardship.
- Worship.

For each value, we listed a brief definition along with the Scripture references that provide its biblical foundation. We then created a reflection section that identifies *ventures* and *vampires* for each value. Here's how we defined those terms:

- Venture—An undertaking involving some risk in expectation of gain.
- Vampire—Something dead that sucks the life blood from something living.

These words are a bit dramatic, but they reinforce the reality that our actions must either build our spiritual life or drain it. Being aware of what gives life to our values and what sucks life from them helps us to be proactive in making the best choices in any given situation.

As an example, here is how we define the value *Worship*. (The rest are listed in Appendix A.)

> We believe that we were created to worship God the Father, Son, and Holy Spirit. We worship God as we come together in public services, in smaller settings, and in private devotional times. We worship God when we submit ourselves to Him. The focus of our worship is not ourselves but God.
>
> 1 Chron. 16:29; Ps. 29:1–2; 63:4–5; 95:1–8; 100:1–2; 135:1–3; Isa. 6:1–4; Luke 4:8; John 4:23–24; Acts 2:42–47; Rom. 1:20–23; 12:1; Eph. 5:19–20; Phil. 3:3; Heb. 10:25; Rev. 4:3–11; 7:9–12.

VALUE VENTURES

____ I spend time alone in worship—reading God's Word, praying, listening to Christian music, meditating, and so on.

____ I come prepared to enter into times of public worship.
– Prayed Up

____ I engage in all the dimensions of worship—celebration, reflection, repentance, etc.—regardless of personal preference.

____ I attend public worship almost weekly, making it a priority.

VALUE VAMPIRES

____ I am a spectator and critic, evaluating how well the people up front are doing.

_____ I leave a service asking "Did I like it?" rather than "What did I offer to God today?"

_____ I limit my expressions of worship to the comfortable and familiar rather than seeking what God desires of me.

_____ I demean forms of worship that I experience as less meaningful even if others experience them as significant.

By providing a list of ventures and vampires for each value, we offer each member an opportunity to evaluate the degree to which that value is present in his or her life.

Our beliefs and values form the heart of our church's covenant with God. When a company takes its annual inventory, it limits or shuts down other activities. While this temporarily slows productivity, that company understands that an accurate inventory is a tool for evaluating its current condition. Periodically God will slow down leaders or congregations so they can "take inventory"—evaluate the current condition of their beliefs and behaviors.

For the people of Israel, the renewal of their covenant with God was a proactive step toward avoiding the temptation to make covenants with the people of the land (Ex. 23:32). So the timing of their circumcision, which symbolized their loyalty to the covenant, was perfect. They were now in the land, seeing first hand the people who were there and the gods that they worshiped. The renewal of the covenant was a spiritual vaccination that would strengthen their resistance to other gods.

CONCLUSION

The significance of Israel's circumcision might be stated this way:

Repentance + Reliance + Renewal = **Release of God's power through His promises**

At Kentwood Community Church, we are living the reality of this formula right now as we seek to reach more people by becoming culturally diverse as a congregation. The population of our neighborhood is about 22 percent minority while our congregation is about 1 percent minority. Like many aging churches, ours is mostly a drive-in congregation, and we sense a growing disconnection with our closest neighbors.

We've tried to identify areas of prejudice and racism that require repentance. We're relying on God to bring leaders from many cultures who can help us reach out to all people more effectively. And we're asking God to renew our beliefs and behaviors so that we will genuinely welcome all people. As we are faithful in these areas, we've begun to witness the release of God's power based on His promise to gather in heaven people from every tribe, language, and people. As we move further and further beyond ourselves, relying ever more fully on God's power, we're expecting to have a bit of heaven on earth as we worship together!

PERSONAL REFLECTION

1. Circumcision was a tangible expression of allegiance to God's covenant with Israel. What are some tangible ways in which we express our allegiance to God today?

2. Is God speaking to you about any area that requires personal repentance?

3. Emotional intelligence is the ability to honestly assess and then discipline oneself to make needed changes. Which of your current attitudes and actions would you identify as strengths? As weaknesses?

4. Which of your current attitudes and actions might be improved with greater self-discipline?

5. In which areas of your life do you find it easiest to rely upon God? In which is it most difficult?

6. What are some of your personal core values?

Inventory for Spiritual Leaders

1. Are there any areas of personal or congregational repentance that God is speaking to me about?

2. What services or events have led to significant change in our ministry or church?

3. When was the time in my ministry when I relied upon God the most? How did I feel at that time? What were its results?

4. Have we clarified and communicated our core beliefs?

5. Have we clarified and communicated our core values?

6. Choose one of the core values of your ministry. List some of the ventures that reinforce it. What are some of the vampires that drain the life out of it?

Joshua's Journal

Lord, I want to give my full allegiance to You. Please help me to consistently identify anything that stands in the way of my full devotion. Help me not only to repent of it but also to rely fully upon You for daily victory over it. Help me to stretch my faith so that I don't live by self-reliance but move to the place where I must rely upon your power and promises. May my beliefs and behavior be completely aligned with Your Word, Heavenly Father. Amen.

CHAPTER THREE

God's Power for God's Purpose

—⟋⟋⟍—

> **STALL FACTOR:** Lack of power.
> **FORWARD STEP:** Pursue God relentlessly.

John Wesley is one of my heroes. Above my desk I've mounted a prayer that I believe captures the secret of his success. It's a prayer of yieldedness.

I am no longer my own, but thine.

Put me to what thou wilt, rank me with whom thou wilt.

Put me to doing, put me to suffering.

Let me be employed by thee or laid aside for thee,

Exalted for thee or brought low by thee.

Let me be full, let me be empty.

Our power is not so much in us as through us.

—Harry Emerson Fosdick

The LORD	Let me have all things, let me have nothing.
Almighty has	I freely and heartily yield all things to thy
sworn, 'Surely, as	pleasure and disposal.
I have planned, so	And now, O glorious and blessed God,
it will be, and as	Father, Son, and Holy Spirit.
I have purposed,	Thou are mine, and I am thine.
so it will stand.	So be it. Amen.

—Isaiah 14:24

I incorporate Wesley's emphasis on yieldedness as the exclamation point in my own pattern of prayer. My personal prayers generally follow this model:

P Praising God for who He is and how He works.

R Repenting of anything that displeases God and resolving to bear the fruit of repentance.

A Asking, seeking, knocking. Persistently pursuing all that is within God's will to give.

Y Yielding all that I am and have to God's will.

As I yield my life to God at the conclusion of each prayer, I get on my knees (if I'm not there already) in a posture of submission and recall Wesley's prayer of complete abandonment to the purposes of God.

Every movement of God starts in a meeting with God. Every movement of God is sustained by meeting with God. So it's no surprise that after entering the Promised Land, Joshua's first encounter was not with the enemy but with an emissary of God. "Now when Joshua was near Jericho, he looked up and saw a man standing in front of him with a drawn sword in his hand" (Josh. 5:13).

The identification of this "man" has been the subject of much speculation. Was it a theophany, God appearing in human form? Was it a Christophany, Christ appearing in human form? Was it an angel?

My choice? It was an angel. Other places in Scripture record the employment of angels for similar missions. I believe Joshua's encounter with this man, and the message he conveyed, would have reminded Joshua of his mentor, Moses. God had promised Joshua, "No one will be able to stand up against you all the days of your life. As I was with Moses, so I will be with you; I will never leave you or forsake you" (Josh. 1:5).

During his brief time as the point person in this movement of God, Joshua had already had many experiences that paralleled the life of Moses. Moses' commission to Joshua, "Be strong and courageous" (Deut. 31:23), had been repeated three times by God Himself (Josh. 1:6, 7, 9). The leaders had pledged to Joshua, "Just as we fully obeyed Moses, so we will obey you. Only may the LORD be with you as he was with Moses" (Josh. 1:17). By God's miraculous provision Joshua had led the people across the Jordan River (Josh. 3:15–17) just as Moses had led the people through the Red Sea (Exod. 14:21–22).

Now Joshua experienced his own "holy ground" encounter (Josh. 5:13–15) with God. Undoubtedly, Moses had told his protégé the story of his burning bush experience (Exod. 3:2–10). An angel of the Lord had appeared to Moses within the flames of a burning bush. His message to Moses began with the words "Take off your sandals, for the place where you are standing is holy ground." That message was almost word-for-word the same as the message Joshua received from his mysterious visitor (Josh. 5:15).

Was this the angel that God had promised would go before them into the Promised Land (Exod. 23:20–23; also 32:34; 33:2)? If so, Joshua well understood that the people of Israel were to "pay attention to him and listen to what he says [and] not rebel against him."

Joshua had the presence of mind to ask the man two questions. Much of the wisdom needed for leadership can be found in asking the right questions. When I entered my ministry, I thought that 99 percent of leadership was having the right answers. The more I lead, however, the more I realize that the real task of a leader is to ask the right questions and then carefully listen for the answers. That's true whether I'm seeking wisdom from God, mentors, team members, or seekers.

We recently searched for a new staff member. Asking the right questions played a crucial role in that process.

- We asked God for a clear vision of the strategy needed in this ministry area and the personal profile that would match that strategy.

- We asked other leaders to review our proposed profile and listened to their suggestions for refinement.

- We asked the interview team to list questions that would determine whether an individual fit the profile and was capable of implementing the strategy.

- We asked questions of the candidates to reveal whether they were a good fit for the position we were seeking to fill.

Leading involves focused listening, and good questions bring that focus.

When we're in a hurry, it's hard to listen and easy to jump to conclusions. Slow-motion times can create a context in which we listen to God and others more fully. For years now I've benefited from the book *Margin*. The author, Richard Swenson, is a medical doctor who identifies four "gears" in our pace of life.[1]

Overdrive. We operate in overdrive when life's demands require heroic expenditures of energy, causing the release of adrenaline within the body. This gear is intended to be used only on rare occasions, but it is where many people spend the majority of their lives. Running too long in overdrive creates an "adrenaline addiction" (and maybe a caffeine addiction as well!).

Drive. Drive is the gear in which we work and play most of the time. Most of the activities of life are enjoyed in this gear.

Slow. Slow is the gear most conducive to building deep and intimate relationships. Without the rush of adrenaline and activity, we are able to listen more fully.

Park. Park is a full stop. This is the gear in which we best listen to God. Most people know that, which is why we call our moments of communion with God "quiet time." The Psalmist speaks often of the power that is gained by heeding God's call to "be still and know that I am God."

Swenson observes that our society, with its emphasis on productivity and activity, increasingly pressures people to live in drive and overdrive, and rarely allows them to operate in slow or park. This has produced a traumatic effect on the relational and spiritual lives of many who are too busy or burned out to develop intimacy with God or others.

If individuals have gears, do churches also? We are energized by the times of dramatic growth and transition that require us to shift into overdrive. But if we live and lead in that gear too long we may diminish our capacity to sense and obey the leading of God's Spirit. As leaders, if we know we are about to embark on a time that will require us to gear up, we should be especially careful to listen to God. We must be still with God before we speed up for Him.

Joshua had some alone time with God's representative just before the battles began. The questions Joshua asked of him zero in on the heart of spiritual leadership. The first is the *power question*; second is the *purpose* question; both are important.

Kevin Myers, a close friend and pastor of a thriving church in Atlanta, Georgia, teaches that "God's calling is where God's power and God's purpose come together in your life." God gives His power only for His purpose—He doesn't give us His power to pursue our own dreams. And God's purpose can only be accomplished with His power—if we try to fulfill God's mission in our own strength, we'll burn out long before we finish. The intersection of God's power and God's purpose causes His kingdom to come and will be done on earth as it is in heaven.

THE POWER QUESTION

Joshua looked up to notice a man standing in front of him. The drawn sword in the man's hand was an unmistakable symbol of power. Joshua's question, "Are you for us or for our enemies?" was certainly a good place to begin. If a well-armed warrior suddenly appeared in front of me, I'd sure want to know whose side he was on!

The man, however, didn't provide a direct answer. He wasn't evasive; in fact, his response was authoritative. He didn't answer this power question simply because it was framed in the wrong way.

Joshua's question made the people of God its point of reference—"Are you for *us* or for *our* enemies?" The reply changed that point of reference to God—"Neither . . . but as a commander of the army of the LORD I have now come." God doesn't choose sides with us. Rather, He leaves us with a question—will we side with Him?

One of my pet peeves is Christian clichés that are sentimentally appealing but theologically inaccurate. One such phrase is "God is my copilot." It conjures an image of the Christian as being in control while God is simply along for the ride, ready to help in case of emergency. The truth is, God is my pilot, and more often than not He instructs me to keep my hands off the controls!

Too many church disputes lead to members taking sides, acting like the church belongs to them. They spiritualize their actions by claiming that God is on *their* side. Everyone involved in such squabbling needs a strong reminder that the Church belongs to God—He is at the center and should be given complete control. Maybe the "man with a drawn sword" should show up at some congregational meetings!

The answer this man gave to Joshua provides the keys to releasing God's power in the life of a leader.

KEY NUMBER ONE: KNOW YOUR ROLE

The man identified himself as "commander of the army of the LORD." I wonder if Joshua had the same title on his own business card! Joshua must have been surprised that the man's job description was so similar, if not identical, to the role he envisioned for himself. For many years Joshua had been Moses' aide. That's how he's identified as the book of Joshua begins (1:1). When Moses died, Joshua was placed in the role of leader. He is the one who gave orders to the officers (1:10), and what do you call the person who does that? Commander. Now Joshua encountered another commander, the angelic "commander of the army of the LORD."

This conversation, coming as it did before the first military conflict, was an opportunity for role clarification. To be successful in any God-honoring objective, leaders must know the role God is calling them to play. And roles must not be confused with titles. For over twenty years my title has been Senior Pastor, and over that time my role has been adjusted frequently.

- Filler of the big shoes left behind by the founding pastor (1981).
- Builder of facilities (1983).
- Communicator of vision to increasing numbers of people joining us for a variety of reasons (1983 and following).
- Manager of staff (1984 and following).
- Leader of staff (1990 and following).
- Mentor to younger leaders (currently).

Making role adjustments can take time. A leader may need the counsel of trusted colleagues even to see that it's time for role refocusing to take place. Our January 2000 board retreat was just such a time for me. Our board lovingly and courageously identified the roles that needed to be filled in order to move forward in our God-given mission. As much as possible, they set aside their personal feelings about the people who currently filled those in order to objectively define role requirements.

They began with the role of the senior pastor. The person currently filling that role was me! I'd love to tell you that I was completely nondefensive during the process. In reality, I vacillated between commitment to role refocusing, which I knew was necessary, and preoccupation with my own desires.

The board asked (again, the power of the right questions), "In light of our mission and vision, what do we need from the senior pastor of Kentwood Community Church?" They listed several abilities that were needed and some characteristics to be avoided:

Needed

- Leadership of platform ministry, exhibiting the "spirit and truth" of true worship.

- Vision clarification and communication. The vision must become specific and strategic so that it can be implemented and measured.

- Leadership development, including both key staff and lay individuals to fulfill the point-person roles in every area of vision pursuit.

To Be Avoided

- Personally providing necessary pastoral care and counseling for a large percentage of the congregation. The goal is to be an equipper of caregivers rather than a doer of care ministry, with a few exceptions.

- Micromanaging personnel and programming. People are to be empowered to lead, and while vision alignment is critical, there must be freedom to pursue the vision in a style that fits each leader.

Having objectively defined the role of the senior pastor, the board then asked a set of intimidating questions—at least they seemed so to me! They asked:

- Do Wayne Schmidt's strengths correspond with the abilities that we need?

- Does he have the potential to develop any skill sets that he is presently lacking?

- Can he discipline himself to avoid the things that would distract him from his role?

Then I had to examine myself. I asked:

- Is the role described here one to which God is calling me?

- Am I motivated to acquire the new skills that this changed role requires?

- Should I seek a role elsewhere that better fits my God-given passions and abilities?

After prayer and discussion, both the board and I discerned that God was leading me to grow into the role as presently described.

Part of what motivated me to submit to the process was two pastoral "train wrecks" in nearby churches. Each of the pastors had served his congregation well for many years. Each congregation had grown from fewer than 200 to more than 500 in weekly attendance, so it wasn't a matter of getting stuck at the infamous 200 Barrier. Each pastor, however, led his church by being an omnipresent caregiver and participant in every ministry committee. As gifted as they were (they sustained this pace much longer than most pastors could have), they reached their inevitable limits. They could no longer meet every need or personally guide every decision. Nor could they adjust, even though their boards repeatedly sought to assist them, to the role requirements of a senior pastor in congregations of the current size and situation. Their inability to refocus their roles resulted in several years of frustrated service, which culminated in forced resignations. That was painful for all involved because these men were deeply loved yet unwilling or unable to adjust to the changed requirements of their pastoral roles.

Their experiences forged a conviction within me that I must rise to the challenge of role refocusing—or resign. I've had the privilege of serving Kentwood Community Church for more than two decades in a relationship that God has made beneficial for both the church and me. I resolved that I will not subtly sabotage needed changes just to preserve my place on the organizational chart. To do so would result in diminished fruitfulness, or even worse, division within the church. It may be difficult. God may need to provide some slow-motion time for me to understand and adjust. But I will grow or I will go.

Of course, role refocusing would be easier if pastors filled only one role. We don't. In my life I juggle the roles of disciple, husband, father, friend, pastor, and several others. Within my role as pastor I juggle the roles of worship leader, vision communicator, and leadership developer. It may be that only one of those roles needs to be refocused, or perhaps all of them do.

The more permanent a role is, the more difficult it is to refocus. Most of us can adjust to new roles when we know they are temporary. For instance, I serve on several leadership teams, and on each of those teams I fill a different role. Those roles have fewer expectations, they last only for limited time, and they're less central to my call to ministry than the role of senior pastor. That makes them much easier to adjust or even resign.

What is the key to making successful role adjustments? In my own life, it has been resisting the temptation to pursue self-interest in order to be a servant leader. Jesus' disciples once scrambled for the roles they thought were ideal for themselves. He challenged them with these words: "If you want to be the greatest, you must be the servant of all" (Mk. 10:43 paraphrase). As followers of Christ we are instructed, "Each of you should look not only to your own interests, but also to the interests of others" (Phil. 2:4). Paul goes on to describe how Jesus led others by providing the ultimate example of servant leadership—He sacrificed His life. A movement of God always requires servant leaders.

We are diligently seeking to promote and preserve a culture of servant leadership at Kentwood Community Church. When we see evidence of that, we celebrate it. When we see preoccupation with self-interest, we confront it. We realize that if we don't deal with it, God may send an angel with a drawn sword to help us get it right.

KEY NUMBER TWO: KNOWING YOUR RESOURCES

"Are you for us or our enemies?" Joshua asked. But the question was too limiting. It confined all impending battles to involvement by two earthly armies. The man's answer—that he belongs to neither earthly army but to the "army of the LORD"—is a reminder of the reality of spiritual warfare.

A movement of God always involves two armies—the human and the divine. A movement of God always invites the opposition of two enemies—the human and the demonic. So forward movement always requires spiritual leaders to faithfully fulfill their roles and humbly pray for God's resources.

Joshua's encounter with this man must have prompted a forty-year flashback. Moses had commanded Joshua to go out with some of the men of Israel to fight the Amalekites (Exod. 17:8–15). Moses stood atop a nearby hill with the staff of God in his hands. This staff had been the instrument that brought God's plagues upon Egypt, winning the release of the Hebrew people from Egypt. As long as Moses held up the staff, the Israelites dominated. But as Moses tired and lowered his hands, the tide turned against them. Finally, Moses sat down on a stone while Aaron and Hur supported his hands, holding the staff high. Joshua defeated the Amalekites in battle because the God of Israel defeated the Amalekites with the staff. Moses commemorated this powerful partnership with an altar called "The LORD Is My Banner." Moses recognized that the necessary resources were released into hands that were lifted to the throne of the Lord.

Periodically we need to be reminded that "our struggle is not against flesh and blood, but against the rulers, against the authorities, against the powers of this dark world and against the spiritual forces of evil in the heavenly realms" (Eph. 6:12). So we're to be alert and keep on praying, regularly lifting our hands to the throne of the Lord for the resources needed for victory.

When I need a reminder of God's provision, my flashback doesn't go back forty years, and the event I recall did not result in the construction of an altar. It was during 1983 when one of my roles as senior pastor was to help with the construction of our first facility. It was a summer Saturday afternoon, hot and humid. I was physically pounding nails while mentally rehearsing the next day's sermon. There were supposed to have been many volunteers that day, but nobody showed up. Tired, alone, overwhelmed—I was the perfect candidate for discouragement.

Finally, I slumped in the corner of the room. It happened to be the ladies' room, and it's hard for me to admit that one of my greatest encounters with God took place in a women's restroom! Salty tears streamed down my sweaty face, which mixed with sawdust as I wiped them away. I was having an Elijah-style pity party—I was the only one left to do God's work. At that moment my dad walked in, and I launched into a tale of woe about how the whole church was being carried on my shoulders.

At that moment, my heavenly Father spoke through my earthly father. He said, "It's not your church; it's God's church. And it won't be built in your strength, but His strength. You have to do your part, but keep your hands off His part."

Ouch.

There was more. "If you keep those things straight," Dad promised, "God will never give you more than you can bear." Though I was initially resistant, I knew he was right. The burden began to lighten, and peace settled in.

Sometimes God slows us down to remind us that His purposes can only be accomplished with His power. The battle will only be won if the commander of His heavenly army shows up with sword in hand.

THE PURPOSE QUESTION

Joshua fell facedown in reverence for the commander of the Lord's army. A good response. We deal with God always from a position of submission. Then Joshua asked a second question, better framed than the first: "What message does my LORD have for his servant?" It was the question of purpose. Joshua was ready to take orders from the Lord.

A MOVEMENT HAS A MISSION

In 1979 I was completing undergraduate work at Indiana Wesleyan University (then Marion College). During that year, a good friend, Dennis Jackson, entered into a prayer partnership with me. We met every Friday morning at 6:00 A.M. to seek God's mission for my life upon completion of this stage of education. I have found that God usually reveals His will first in general terms, then gives specific focus gradually. I call this the *Focus Funnel*.

FOCUS FUNNEL

As we began to pray for clarity, I asked a series of questions:

"Am I to go on to seminary or enter ministry?" The answer—ministry.

"Am I to pursue parachurch ministry or local church ministry?" The answer—local church ministry.

"Am I to serve an existing church or to be involved in planting a church?" The answer—be involved in planting a church.

"Is there a particular place I'm to plant?" The answer—southeastern Grand Rapids.

Now these answers were not audible, but I clearly sensed that there was a specific direction I should pursue unless God closed the doors. So when the leader of our denomination for West Michigan visited the campus, I shared my sense of God's leading with him. That leader, Vaughn Drummonds, responded by laughing out loud!

He was laughing because the previous week, completely unknown to me, he had sat in the living room of Dick Wynn in Kentwood, a southeastern suburb of Grand Rapids, where Dick said, "If you find the right young man to work with me, I will serve as part-time senior pastor to plant a church in Kentwood." Dick, who served full-time with Youth for Christ, had counseled me as I clarified my initial call to ministry. Now God was clearly leading us to work together! He would continue serving Youth for Christ and give part-time leadership as I became a full-time assistant pastor.

Sensing God's mission was not a one-time event. I aim to begin each day on my knees, asking that God's calling will be accomplished in my life in the next twenty-four hours. I want to live that day in the place where His power and purpose intersect. In a face-down posture of submission I list the top priorities in my life. First among them is this:

> To experience increasing intimacy with God in tandem with greater clarity, intensity, and tenacity in pursuing His calling upon my life.

The latter half of my first priority focuses on God's mission for my life.

- *Clarity.* I lift before God each of the three roles that are my present responsibility as senior pastor. I ask God to reveal what is *on purpose* and remove from me what is *off purpose* with His calling.

- *Intensity.* I ask God's Spirit to fill me with energy and passion for that day's pursuits. I express my longing to keep in step with His Spirit so that my energy won't be squandered on low priorities but focused on what matters.

- *Tenacity.* I seek God's power to persevere, knowing that this will both develop my character and sustain my contribution to His mission.

When I slow down enough to begin the day this way, God's mission is clear in my mind and my motivation is strong. When I rush to begin my day and omit this time, the sense of His presence is more distant and my sense of His purpose less well defined.

Our leaders of our church recently re-examined our mission. The slower motion days of 2001 allowed us to see God's calling more clearly. I know that there are at least a hundred definitions for mission and vision, and ceaseless arguments over which is correct. We chose the definitions that worked best for us:

Mission—What we *must do* to fulfill God's purpose for us.

Vision—What we *will see* as God's purpose is fulfilled through us.

Adopting those definitions led us to create a mission statement that is brief and easily communicated, and a vision statement that is longer and more detailed.

OUR MISSION

The mission of Kentwood Community Church is to obey Christ by reaching out to spiritually lost people and raising up fully committed believers who love God completely and others unconditionally.

Our mission is unashamedly Christ-centered in a culture where the name *god* can be attached to nearly anything yet the name of Christ is considered divisive. Our mission is lived out in obedience to Jesus Christ. It's involves *reaching out* to spiritually lost people (the Great Commission— Matt. 28:18–20) and *raising up* fully committed believers who love God completely and others unconditionally (the Great Commandment— Mark 12:30–31). Our mission is simple enough to be reduced to a motto or even a logo—Reaching Out and Raising Up—R & R. When our mission functions at its fullest, it feeds on itself—we reach out to people, raise them up as fully committed believers who in turn reach out to others, who are in turn raised up. . . . The cycle goes on.

Our vision statement is more complex (see complete text in Appendix B). It identifies the attitudes and actions we'll observe as we incarnate the mission in believers who belong to Kentwood Community Church. Here's an example, taken from our vision for *serving:*

> We dream of every believer serving as part of the body of Christ and under the Lordship of Christ. *Where* we serve is shaped by our passions, *what* we do utilizes our spiritual gifts, and *how* we serve is influenced by our personal style. More than volunteers who give of something that belongs to us, we are ministers who serve recognizing all we are and have belongs to God. We dream of every believer exercising stewardship of their time, talents, and money, permitting an uninterrupted flow of resources from God through believers to benefit His kingdom.

Joshua's reverent submission to the commander of the Lord's army evinces his willingness to join God's mission rather than a desire to coax God to adopt Joshua's plans. Joshua's attitude manifests the insight captured so powerfully by Henry Blackaby in the book *Experiencing God.* Blackaby says that we are to discover what God is doing and join Him where He is already at work. We're not to twist God's arm, seeking His blessing on what we've already decided to do. A movement of God always follows the mission of God.

A MOVEMENT HAS A MESSAGE

As Joshua fell facedown in reverence, he asked the man "What message does my LORD have for His servant?" Reverence brings receptivity to revelation. Joshua was ready to listen with the heart of a servant. He understood that a true encounter with God must be two-way, involving both asking and listening.

When our church board or staff has reached a defining moment, we often pause to engage in listening prayer. We quiet our hearts and ask

God to communicate a response to some specific question. The question varies depending on the circumstance. It might relate to a problem that needs a solution. It might be a request for guidance at a strategic cross-road. It may be a personnel matter or a question about the direction of a ministry program. First we clearly define the question, then we ask God to remove from our minds any preconceived assumptions and protect us from being swayed by human opinions or, worse yet, suggestions from our enemy, Satan. Finally, we ask that we will hear His "voice." Then we sit in silence. We jot down thoughts that occur to us during prayer. They may be single words, paragraphs, or bits of song or Scripture. In a sense, we are brainstorming through prayer.

After praying, we ask each person to share what he or she sensed from the Lord. We look for themes, trying to identify the concepts that resonate most fully with the group. We take these thoughts into consideration as we form a final decision.

Understand that we don't leave the room and announce to the world, "God told us to. . . ." As Dan Webster put it, "Oral Roberts (the former televangelist), Charlie Manson (the mass murderer), Oprah Winfrey (the talk show host), and Chuck Colson (the founder of Prison Fellowship) all have one thing in common—they all believe that they listen to the voice of God and obey it." Yet we do leave those meetings knowing that quieting our heart before God, listening carefully for His leading and testing what we've heard in the context of community, raises the likelihood that we'll choose the direction God intends for us.

As Joshua listened, the commander replied, "Take off your sandals, for the place where you are standing is holy." Moses received this same message before his mission to Egypt. Now it was given to Joshua before he embarked on his mission in the Promised Land. Joshua responded with obedience.

Not surprisingly, Joshua understood the message the first time God delivered it. A drawn sword is a powerful communication tool! Yet for me, more often than not it takes repeated revelation for God to get through. I'm more like Samuel (1 Sam. 3), who needed to hear the call of God three times before he realized what it was. I am often moving too fast or am too preoccupied to develop the "ears to hear" and "eyes to see" God's revelation.

I am humbled by the fact that God graciously repeats His messages so I can be included in what He is doing. It's painful for me, after finally receiving God's message, to look back over months or even years and see the times God tried to communicate with me but I didn't hear. Hindsight has shown me the need to regularly ask God to make His will plain—and help me get it the first time.

For me, that happens only when I experience a Spirit-generated combination of humility and purity. Without that, I'd never have the tenacity to persevere in my calling. At times I've begged to be released from the responsibilities God has placed upon my shoulders. Rather than giving that release, God nearly always uses those occasions to imprint this truth upon my heart—obedience requires perseverance.

The encounter with God's messenger changed Joshua's life and his leadership. And no wonder. When God's power and God's purpose come together, it's time to take off our sandals. Something holy is about to happen.

PERSONAL REFLECTION

1. In what areas of life do you have to work most diligently to be yielded to God? What steps do you take to achieve that surrender?

2. Do you have a pattern that guides your personal prayer times?

3. List the various roles that you fill personally and professionally. Write a brief statement describing how you seek to honor God in each role.

4. How do you prepare for spiritual warfare (see Eph. 6:10–20)?

5. Do you know your personal mission and message? Write them in one or two paragraphs.

INVENTORY FOR SPIRITUAL LEADERS

1. If effective leadership requires asking the right questions, what are some questions that leaders in your ministry should ask each other about their personal lives? About their ministry endeavors?

2. What distinguishes a servant leader from a self-serving leader? What are the signs that you are growing as a servant leader?

3. How clearly can you describe your current role as a leader? Which of the expectations that accompany that role are you willing to do? Which are you unwilling to do?

4. Can you give a brief statement of the mission of your ministry (what God has called you to do)? Can you give a more detailed statement of the vision of your ministry (what you will see as it becomes reality)?

5. Is your leadership team facing a decision or conflict that listening prayer might help to resolve?

—⟶

JOSHUA'S JOURNAL

Lord, please allow me to experience some "holy ground" moments in my leadership journey. May I understand the ministry role You have for me and submit fully to You so that I might faithfully fill it. May I know the joy of Your power flowing through me to accomplish Your purpose. I want to hear Your still, small voice above everything else that clamors for my attention. Amen.

CHAPTER FOUR

OVERCOMING

OBSTACLES

———〰———

STALL FACTOR:	Failure to build upon God-given victories.
FORWARD STEP:	Exercise your will and strategize solutions.

People seek God's will in many different ways. Among the most common is the open door–closed door approach. That's when we pray, "If it is your will Lord, open the door and give us the courage to walk through it. If it is not your will, close the door so tight that we can't pry it open."

But what if the objective is God's will yet the door is shut tight? That's exactly the position in which Joshua found himself. God had personally revealed to Joshua that it was His will to give the Promised Land to Israel. Yet the first city they were to conquer, Jericho, "was tightly shut up because of the Israelites. No one went out and no one came in" (6:1).

> *The harder the conflict, the more glorious the triumph. What we obtain too cheaply, we esteem too lightly.*
>
> —Thomas Paine

A great door of effective work has opened to me, and there are many who oppose me.

—1 Corinthians 16:9

Spiritual leaders understand that even when a project is God's will there may be obstacles to overcome. Even when we're certain of God's purpose and working in His power we may bump our noses on some closed doors. There are always barriers to victory. They remind us that there are some openings only God can create. They may slow us down a bit as we work and pray to overcome or go around them, but we should not be intimidated by these obstacles or ignore them.

ANALYZING OBSTACLES

Every year each member of our church staff and several of our lay ministers develop their personal ministry action plan (MAP). The MAP is developed in three parts:

M *Momentum goals.* These are the areas having the greatest potential for fruitfulness in the coming year. This should be a short list, focused on investment in the arenas where the most momentum can be generated.

A *Activities.* These are areas of practical faithfulness. They are core ingredients of the position that the staff member or lay minister fills. Their completing doesn't create the most momentum, but their neglect would certainly lead to a loss of momentum.

P *Possibilities.* These are areas worth exploring but dependent upon factors or people beyond our control.

For each momentum goal a *Force Field Analysis* is created. In a left hand column, supporting forces are identified—resources that can be leveraged to achieve the goal. In the right hand column, opposing forces are listed—sources of resistance to achieving the goal.

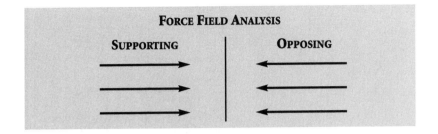

Thorough preparation always reveals that both forces are present. The existence of opposing forces does not indicate the absence of God's will. Rather, it shows where additional prayer, perseverance, and planning may be required.

I'll never forget a conversation I had with a pastor one day in my office. He knew that it was God's will for his church to relocate. Ideal property had been purchased, and he had the credibility to lead the transition. He went on to share that he had one board member who was "a little hesitant" and that 10 percent of his congregation was fairly resistant to the change. His decision: to pray that there would be complete unanimity in the board and congregation as an indication that it was God's will to relocate. That unanimity never materialized, and 90 percent of the congregation, as well as the progress of the church, were held captive by a hesitant or resistant few. Discontentment grew, that pastor left, and a new pastor was called, who led the congregation to relocate. Had the church become completely unified around the relocation? No. The new pastor did a force field analysis, rightly determined that the supportive forces exceeded the opposing forces, and led them forward. A few members left, but many more people have been reached for Christ.

Making the decision to move forward, however, is not merely a matter of adding up the numbers. There's another factor in the equation.

Let's imagine Joshua sitting down on a rock and developing a force field analysis.

SUPPORTING FORCES	OPPOSING FORCES
God's promise of deliverance (6:2)	City tightly shut up (6:1)
Willing spiritual leaders (6:6)	Opposing king and fighting men (6:2)
United people (6:7)	Troops with no previous battle experience

His list appears to be balanced—the number of supporting forces equal the number of opposing forces. So what made the difference for Joshua, giving him the confidence to move ahead? "Then the LORD said to Joshua . . ." (6:2). He heard what God had to say.

God's voice is the scale tipper in any spiritual decision. Joshua had initiated this movement into the Promised Land in response to the voice of God. Repeatedly God had instructed Joshua to "be strong and courageous" (1:6–9) in conquering the land. Now Joshua had, once again, personally communicated with God. Responding to God's personal promise was the key not only to initiating this movement but also to continuing it. God didn't stop speaking to Joshua, and Joshua didn't stop listening!

DEFINING STRATEGIES

God spoke to Joshua before anyone else. That's the way God often works with leaders. He reveals His goals, and the steps to take in reaching them, to the leader first. That leader gets the message earlier and clearer than the rest of the people. This is both God's gift to the leader and the burden a leader must bear.

SEEING THE GOD-GIVEN GOAL

I've often heard spiritual leaders say something like this: "It's so clear to me; why can't anybody else see it?" One reason is that the leader usually has a vantage point to see the whole picture while others see only their part in the picture. That leader can look over the forest, while others "can't see the forest for the trees" because they are so deeply involved in one area of ministry. Another reason is that leaders see both the possibilities and the problems while others may be either overwhelmed by the problems or enamored with the possibilities and be unable to realistically imagine the outcome. The capacity to sense the vision earlier and clearer than others contributes to the loneliness of a leader.

By God's design, the leader is granted the privilege of seeing things others are yet to see, and seeing them with greater clarity. God empowers leaders to see what others don't, then commissions those leaders to help others see and act upon the vision.

What did this "supernatural seeing" reveal to Joshua? "See, I have delivered Jericho into your hands, along with its king and its fighting men" (6:2). What would Joshua have seen physically at this point? A walled city filled with fighting men, commanded by a king. Nothing but opposition. What did he see supernaturally? He saw God delivering the city, its king, and its fighting men into Israel's hands. Leaders see what others don't. Where others see obstacles and opposition, God reveals opportunity.

The question for Joshua, and for any spiritual leader, is which vision to trust—the physical or the spiritual. Do we have spiritual "eyes to see" and "ears to hear" what God is saying to us? For Joshua, this was not a matter of fabricating a goal to pursue and framing it in the words "God told me." This was God's promise, which He had given before, that He would give victory. *Deliverer* is a common biblical image of God. Sometimes God delivers us from things (Egypt), while at other times He delivers things to us (Jericho). In this case, the God-given goal was the deliverance of Jericho into the hands of His people as a first step in a long-term plan to conquer the Promised Land.

When Joshua heard personally from God, he understood his role as a spiritual leader. Spiritual leadership is not a matter of conquering territory. It is a matter of positioning God's people to receive what God has promised to them. The leader must help God's people both to see God's goal and to act in God's power to reach it.

DEFINING THE STRATEGY FOR VICTORY

Joshua had been given his mission. The specific steps to accomplishing that mission had been specified in a clear vision. The first of those steps had been crystallized into an immediate goal. To see and communicate the mission, vision, and goal is the responsibility of every spiritual leader charged with managing a movement of God. And there is one more element required for success. A strategy for reaching each goal must be identified.

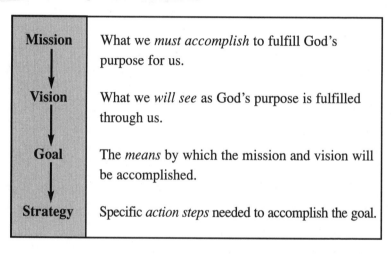

Mission	What we *must accomplish* to fulfill God's purpose for us.
Vision	What we *will see* as God's purpose is fulfilled through us.
Goal	The *means* by which the mission and vision will be accomplished.
Strategy	Specific *action steps* needed to accomplish the goal.

The strategy was the last element of the plan revealed to Joshua. And an unusual strategy it was. Here are the action steps that God indicated:

March around the city once with all the armed men. Do this for six days. Have the seven priests carry trumpets of rams' horns in front of the ark. On the seventh day, march around the city seven times, with the priests blowing the trumpets. When you hear them sound a long blast on the trumpets, have all the people give a loud shout; then the wall of the city will collapse and the people will go up, every man straight in (Josh. 6:3–5).

What kind of strategy is this? The Israelites must have wondered whether it was the product of inspiration or insanity! It was certainly a strategy that had never been used before, nor would be again. It was a faith-based plan that involved a series of actions that were tailor made to reach the goal in a way that could bring glory only to God. When spiritual strategies are used, the goal is reached and God is revered.

The more one progresses in the development of a God-given calling, the more unique it becomes. The mission of our church is based on the Great Commission (Matt. 28:18–20) and the Great Commandment (Mark 12:30–31). The key components, Reaching Out and Raising Up, are biblically sound and could be generally applied to thousands of churches. Our vision, however, reflects our situation more specifically. Our goals are nearly unique, probably applicable only to this congregation. Our strategies, therefore, are highly individualized. That's the way it must be with any congregation. Strategies are highly specialized because the steps a church takes to reach its goals will be shaped by the answers to these personalized questions:

- What goals is God leading us to accomplish?

- What resources are available to us?

- What is unique about our history and culture that will affect the way our actions are perceived and received?

- What is unique about our ministry context?

- Do our proposed action steps align with our church's values and beliefs?

In answering these questions, the highest compliment any leader can receive is the one extended to the men of Issachar, "who understood the times and knew what Israel should do." A spiritual leader must understand the uniqueness of his or her situation and then determine which steps should be taken to reach the God-given goal.

One of the two key objectives of our church's mission is to reach out. Outreach can be accomplished through a variety of strategies.

The strategy we use may be illustrated by an outstretched hand, with each finger representing one dimension of the plan.

KENTWOOD COMMUNITY CHURCH OUTREACH STRATEGY

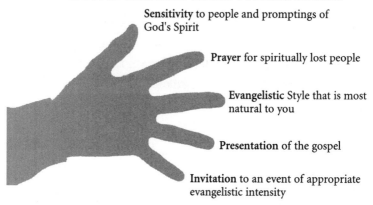

Sensitivity to people and promptings of God's Spirit

Prayer for spiritually lost people

Evangelistic Style that is most natural to you

Presentation of the gospel

Invitation to an event of appropriate evangelistic intensity

Thumb. The thumb reminds us to increase our awareness of divine moments of opportunity by raising our sensitivity to God and others. We're mystified as to why some Christians go months or years (and some a whole lifetime!) without having an opportunity to share the gospel while others regularly see opportune moments. I believe those opportunities come as we are in tune to the Spirit and dialed-in to the needs of others. Intentionally raising our awareness in these two areas empowers us to see and seize more opportunities.

First Finger. The first finger represents intentional and regular prayer for people who are spiritually lost. We call this our Four Heaven's Sake List. We encourage everyone in our congregation to keep such a list, identifying at least four people for whom they will pray regularly.

Second Finger. The second finger represents our evangelistic style. The course *The Contagious Christian* has helped many people identify their style of sharing the gospel. Some are intellectual in their approach, others confrontational, invitational, or some other style. There are a number of ways to approach evangelism. When people work within their own style, they are more likely to be effective.

Third Finger. The third finger is a reminder that we must know a simple way to present the gospel. If a believer can verbally explain or draw on a dinner napkin the simple steps to entering a personal relationship with Jesus Christ, he or she will be prepared to offer an invitation when the time comes.

Fourth Finger. The fourth finger represents invitation. We encourage members to invite spiritually lost friends to events that have an evangelistic intensity appropriate for their spiritual journey. We've developed a scale of 1–5 to communicate the evangelistic intensity of our ministries. A "1" event is low intensity, a fun event without prayer or preaching. A "5" event is a high intensity event at which we make a compelling presentation of the options of eternal life in heaven or hell, then offer an invitation and await a response. It's up to members to discern which level of intensity will help their friends to take the next step.

So our strategy for outreach reflects our unique situation and helps us see clearly what we need to do in order to equip others to participate in the mission of reaching out.

IMPLEMENTING THE STRATEGY EFFECTIVELY

A study of the strategy given to Joshua shouldn't prompt us to organize a march. The strategy was unique to the situation. But there are characteristics of this strategy that can be applied to any movement of the people of God.

LEADERSHIP CROSS-SECTION

First, it was communicated to and elicited commitment from a cross-section of leaders. The first group Joshua called for were the priests (6:6–7). These spiritual leaders had fresh faith because of the miraculous leadership they had recently provided in crossing the Jordan (3:14–4:18). Joshua also involved the armed guard (6:7, 9), who would serve as a wall of protection around the priests and the ark of the covenant. This march would involve the participation of all leaders in ways that were consistent with their roles.

Implementation of a sound strategy begins with the identification of influential people within the church. This identification is not an act of favoritism, but is a recognition that there are "opinion leaders" in every organization who are crucial to a strategy's success. For instance, the Pareto Principle, also known as the 80/20 rule, holds that 80 percent of our results comes from 20 percent of our actions. Many churches have found that—

- 80 percent of the income is given by 20 percent of the people.

- 80 percent of the serving is done by 20 percent of the people.

- 80 percent of the prayer is offered by 20 percent of the people.

- 80 percent of the witnessing is accomplished by 20 percent of the people.

So a leader in a church of 200 might ask, "Who are the forty people (20 percent) who are most influential in the life of our church?" I'd recommend that he not publish this list!

Having identified the opinion leaders, there are two questions to consider. First, what is the best way to communicate with them about the steps that are planned? One-on-one? In small groups? By phone? In writing? Second, what type of involvement will be needed from them? Prayer? Feedback? Specific responsibility for implementing some part of the strategy?

When opinion leaders have a connection with the leader of the movement, they take ownership of the initiative.

SYMBOLS

Next, Joshua's God-given strategy was filled with symbols that had significance to the people. The centerpiece of their movement was the ark of the covenant (6:6). This most sacred piece of tabernacle furniture was approximately five feet long, three feet wide, and three feet deep. It signified the Lord's throne and had been the focal point in their movement across the Jordan River (3:3).

The priests were instructed to carry trumpets. These instruments, fashioned from rams' horns, were not musical instruments but were used for signaling in religious and military contexts. Their sound announced the presence of the Lord (2 Sam. 6:15; 1 Chron. 15:28; Zech. 9:14).

The number seven was also used symbolically. Seven priests were to carry trumpets (6:6) and march around the city on seven consecutive days, marching seven times around on the seventh day (6:15). This would certainly call to mind the seven days of creation and the significance of the number seven as a symbol of completion or perfection.

A sound strategy makes use of symbols that are significant to the people. For instance, our vision includes stewardship: "More than volunteers who give of something that belongs to us, we are ministers who serve recognizing all that we are and have belongs to God. We dream of every believer exercising stewardship of their time, talents, and money, permitting an uninterrupted flow of resources from God through believers to benefit His kingdom." So when I teach on financial freedom through biblical stewardship, I use as symbols ten large, colored, interchangeable blocks. Each block represents one tenth of a person's income.

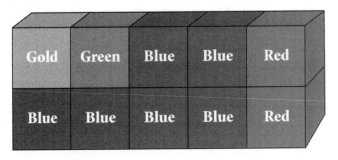

Gold Block   This 10 percent represents the tithe.

Green Block   This 10 percent represents savings.

Blue Blocks   These blocks represent spending.

Red Blocks   These blocks represent debt.

I arrange the blocks in different patterns to represent different financial situations in which people find themselves. Since I've taught on this subject several times, whenever people see the blocks on the platform, they think of the phrase "God's pattern for financial freedom." The blocks have become a significant symbol to our maturing stewards.

BROAD-BASED PARTICIPATION

Third, Joshua's strategy was implemented through broad-based participation by the people. While there were specialized roles for the leaders, everyone had an opportunity to march. Their participation in the march represented their confidence in the strategy that had been revealed to Joshua. It also allowed them to share in the victory that was to be celebrated when the walls of Jericho came down. Later on, when the walls did fall, "everyone charged straight in" (6:20) and joined in devoting the city to the Lord.

God gave the people easy first steps for involvement. "Go for a walk (6:7) . . . keep quiet (6:10) . . . then shout (16)." These steps also developed obedience and perseverance in the people. While the leaders had more complex responsibilities in keeping with their roles, the followers were included. They were given a part that included them without overwhelming them.

A sound strategy identifies easy first steps that allow for broad participation. For instance, when starting another worship service, identify people who will pray for it, serve as ushers, greeters, hosts, or in other roles. Be creative in identifying as many simple roles as possible to provide significant ownership by the greatest number of people.

THE GOD MOMENT

Joshua's strategy identified the critical God moment in the process (6:16). After circling Jericho for the seventh time on the seventh day, the priests were to blow their trumpets and all the people were to shout, "For the LORD has given you the city." At this point every person in the march was undoubtedly praying that God would show up! God always does things in a way that makes it clear that He was responsible and that He alone should receive the glory. The Israelites had done their part; now it was time for God to do His part. This is not to say that God was less present in any other step of the strategy, but that the "table was set" for God to bring victory in a miraculous way—a way that only He could.

A sound strategy will identify the God moment. In a service it might be the open altar time. In a celebration it might be the time when praise is given for what has been accomplished. In a fundraising campaign it might be the moment people are asked to register their prayer-based financial commitment. The God moment in any strategy must be the focus of fervent prayer as leaders and people ask God to reveal Himself in such a way that all who are spiritually sensitive will conclude, "God did something great today."

GIVING GLORY TO GOD

The successful victory brought about by this strategy resulted in the city of Jericho being "devoted to the LORD" (6:17). That process of devotion is unique to the Old Testament, a reflection of the Israelites' system of sacrificial worship. However, what they did physically after their victory is precisely what we should do spiritually, devoting ourselves completely to the Lord. That involves four specific actions. I call them the *motion of devotion.*

ELIMINATION

Devotion involves the elimination of all that is contrary to God. "They devoted the city to the LORD and destroyed with the sword every living thing in it—men and women, young and old, cattle, sheep and donkeys" (6:21). Moses, Joshua's predecessor and mentor, had ordered the Israelites not to leave alive anything that breathes, or those survivors might teach the Israelites to sin and to worship other gods (Deut. 20:16–20). Eliminating them would keep the Israelites from idolatry and its accompanying moral corruption.

Today, being fully devoted to God involves the removing from our lives anything that leads toward idolatry. Idols are God's competitors in our lives, those things that vie for the first place that belongs only to Him. Conquering requires cleansing.

PRESERVATION

Devotion also involves preserving that which is valuable to God. Upon entering Jericho, the Israelites were to keep away from the devoted things, for taking them would bring about one's own destruction and the possibility of wider judgement on the camp of Israel. Everything made of silver, gold, bronze, or iron was to be considered sacred and was to be given to the Lord's treasury (6:18–19). These metals would be used in the creation of sacred objects and places. What was won in warfare would be woven into worship.

While it's vital that we remove from our lives that which is contrary to God, it is equally important that we preserve what He values. This preservation often involves the transformation of things that were once used for earthly purposes so that they may be used for eternal purposes. That phrase "the Lord's treasury" reminds me of a conversation that Jesus had with His followers one day. He wanted them to understand that there are two treasuries. One is earthly. It can be lost and is of little lasting value. The other is heavenly. It can't be lost and has eternal value. Jesus concluded His teaching by saying, "For where your treasure is, there your heart will be also" (Matt. 6:19–21).

COMPLETION

Completion is another aspect of devotion. Devotion involves the completion of all promises we have made to God and others. When Jericho fell, Joshua honored the promise that had been made to Rahab (6:25). Earlier, when Joshua sent spies into the land, they met with Rahab, who recognized that "the LORD your God is God in heaven above and on the earth below" (2:11). When the spies were threatened with capture, they promised that if she would help them escape, all who were in her house would be spared in the coming battle. Rahab was to leave a scarlet cord tied in her window until the Israelites returned, which she did. She and her family were spared and lived among the Israelites as they continued to conquer the land.

Joshua's promise keeping showed that he served a God who keeps His word. It also made clear that the destruction of those living in the land was not undertaken because the Israelites were in some way superior to their enemies. Rather, it was based on the refusal by those enemies to honor God. Rahab was saved because she submitted herself to God's will and participated in it. She placed her faith in God, and she—along with her household—demonstrated that faith by seeking sanctuary in her house as the spies had instructed.

Our personal devotion to God is demonstrated when we honor God's promise of salvation by offering the good news to others. For God does "not [want] anyone to perish, but everyone to come to repentance" (2 Pet. 3:9).

REPUTATION

Finally, devotion involves building God's reputation for glory, not our own. After the victory, Joshua pronounced a solemn oath that focused all attention squarely upon God (6:26). In so doing, he used the day's gain as leverage for lasting commitment.

"The LORD was with Joshua and his fame spread" (6:27). God's victory gave Joshua added credibility with the Israelites, strengthening his leadership credentials for future battle. Leaders must constantly reinvest in the mission, just as a financial investor automatically reinvests a client's dividends to keep his account growing. Leaders are stewards of fame, or credibility, and must invest it well. What is the best reason for being famous? Because it's evident that God is with you. A good reputation is a resource that can be used to create movement in the future.

Recently I read an article entitled the "Seven Laws of Lifelong Growth." I found the second law especially intriguing: "Don't allow your rewards to exceed your investments."[1] This law warns leaders that success can bring financial rewards, recognition, speaking engagements, and writing opportunities—none of which are wrong in and of themselves. But if those rewards become our focus, we'll soon find ourselves playing it safe in order to preserve the perks. A leader must constantly reinvest investment of time, energy, and attention in invigorating the forward movement of God's kingdom.

On this point my accountability partnership has been a great benefit. Each opportunity I receive to travel, speak, or write is screened by my accountability partner before acceptance. First of all, I need to be living a balanced personal life and be consistently reaching my accountability goals. Second, I need to faithfully fulfill my leadership role within the local church to which God has called me. To determine how I'm doing, I use questions based on the motion of devotion.

- Have I consistently eliminated from my life attitudes or actions that are not pleasing to God?

- How well have I preserved the values and priorities that are most precious to God?

- Have I kept the promises that I've made so I do not neglect present commitments in my haste to make new ones?

- Have I reinvested whatever ministry credibility I have gained for God's glory rather than using it personal gain?

If these questions can be answered positively, then the opportunity is screened based on how well it fits with my life calling. That prevents me from accepting opportunities based on the glamour of the location or the size of the honorarium. Instead, I'm able to choose those opportunities that best equip others to increase their positive effect on the lives they touch.

It helps me to picture the motion of devotion as a flywheel.

THE MOTION OF DEVOTION

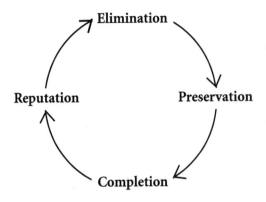

A flywheel starts slowly and is hard to turn at the beginning. It requires a great deal of energy to overcome inertia and make the wheel move. But once it begins, the wheel revolves faster and faster, requiring less and less effort. As my life progresses, I want my acts of devotion to God to occur more readily, even automatically. For many spiritual leaders, the motion of devotion loses momentum as the years go by. God's will is that our devotion should gain momentum with every passing year.

PERSONAL REFLECTION

1. How do you go about seeking God's will for your life? If part of the process involves seeking godly counsel, from whom do you seek it? Why did you choose that person?

2. Jesus said that God reveals His truth and will to those who have "eyes to see" and "ears to hear" (Matt. 11:15; 13:16–17). In what ways can we develop our spiritual "senses" in order to gain more insight and direction from God?

3. What unique ability has God given to you? Of all areas in which you might serve Him, which one makes the best use of your God-given design?

4. What items in your home (pictures or objects, for example) are symbols of your relationship with God?

5. Review the illustration of the hand. How sensitive are you to opportunities to share your faith? Who are the spiritually lost people that you are praying for? What is your evangelistic style? Are you able to share a simple presentation of the gospel? When was the last time you invited someone who is not yet a Christian person to a ministry event?

INVENTORY FOR SPIRITUAL LEADERS

1. Have you created a MAP for your ministry? In which areas can you generate the most momentum for ministry?

2. As a leader, have you ever sensed that God was showing you something that others had yet to see?

3. Review the strategy questions listed in this chapter, answering them in relation to your area of ministry.

4. Who are the people currently making the greatest contribution in your ministry? Who are the emerging leaders who might make a significant contribution in the days ahead? What are you doing to nurture relationships with each of these people?

JOSHUA'S JOURNAL

Lord, help me to discern which doors You are opening for me. Lead me to understand the unique way in which You've designed me and the ways in which I can bear the most fruit. Keep me from being discouraged by the opposing forces that I will undoubtedly experience. May my devotion to You only grow in the days ahead. Amen.

CHAPTER FIVE

THE DEBILITATING DANGER OF DECEPTION

—ᴡᴡ—

> **STALL FACTOR:** Deception.
> **FORWARD STEP:** Acknowledge the truth about yourself and others.

S uccess is dangerous. The greater the victory, the greater the danger. Our greatest victory can set us up for our greatest defeat. That's because success affects our perceptions of the world and ourselves, allowing deception to creep in. When things are happening quickly, it's even easier to be deceived. That's another reason that God sometimes slows us down: to help us see what has really happened and bring debilitating secrets to light.

Joshua and the nation of Israel were coming down from an awesome victory. This was the first time their troops had had to trust God for victory in a military offensive. Their faith positioned them to witness a miracle. The

When our knowing exceeds our sensing, we will no longer be deceived by the illusions of our senses.
—Walter Russell

> *And this is my prayer: that your love may abound more and more in knowledge and depth of insight, so that you may be able to discern what is best and may be pure and blameless until the day of Christ Jesus.*
>
> —Philippians 1:9–10

seemingly impenetrable walls of Jericho had collapsed, and the inhabitants of the city were completely conquered. This significant city was the gateway to the Promised Land. Its defeat marked the beginning of what could only be a series of spectacular victories.

Next up? The city of Ai. No problem. The spies had checked it out and determined that it would offer weak resistance. It wouldn't even be worth sending all the troops (7:3). They recommended that Joshua send two or three thousand troops to conquer the city while the rest enjoyed some down time. Joshua agreed, sent about three thousand men, and waited for the report of victory.

The report he received was not at all what he'd expected. The men of Ai had routed the army of Israel. When they fled, the army of Ai gave chase and killed thirty-six Israelites. The anticipated victory had turned into an unexpected defeat.

Deception is a cancer. It grows inside a seemingly healthy leader. More than one movement of God has been destroyed by the self-deception of its leaders. In Joshua, chapters 7–9, deception creeps into the Israelite camp, distancing them from God and preventing them from enjoying His full blessing.

There are two sources for deception. It can originate within a movement of God based on the presence of disobedience. Or it can come from without based on the absence of discernment.

DECEPTION ON THE INSIDE: THE PRESENCE OF DISOBEDIENCE

The battle of Jericho appeared to have been a complete victory. But that public perception masked the private reality of deception.

Joshua and the other leaders did not yet know what God knew: the "Israelites acted unfaithfully in regard to the devoted things" (7:1).

ROBBING GOD

Because Jericho was the first city conquered in Canaan, it was the firstfruits of the Promised Land. A foundational principle of Scripture is that firstfruits belong to God. They are to be given to Him as an act of worship. In the economy of the ancient world, income came from the land. So God cast the command in agricultural terms: "Bring the best of the firstfruits of your soil to the house of the LORD your God" (Exod. 23:19). When Jericho was conquered, all the silver, gold, bronze, and iron were supposed to have gone into the treasury of the tabernacle. But one man, Achan, had robbed God by taking some of these devoted things for himself. Robbing God of what is rightfully His removes His blessing and replaces it with His anger.

That was true for the Israelites as a nation, and it is also true for God's people individually. Centuries after the defeat at Ai, the last book of the Old Testament recorded God's haunting question "Will a man rob God" (Mal. 3:8)? God then answered His own question: "Yet you rob me." The prophet Malachi carried on a rhetorical debate with God, asking, "How do we rob you?" God answered, "In tithes and offerings." The tithe (one tenth), the firstfruits of their income, was to be devoted to the Lord and brought into His storehouse. God's people were keeping some of that devoted portion for themselves. As a result, they lived under a curse instead of experiencing the fulfillment of God's promise to "throw open the floodgates of heaven and pour out so much blessing that you will not have room enough for it" (3:10).

Robbing God isn't a matter of mugging Him. We don't steal from God by overpowering Him and wresting some possession from His grasp. Robbing God is more like embezzling. An embezzler is someone who's been given access to another person's possessions in order to manage them. But instead of acting faithfully, an embezzler takes the person's possessions for his own use. Incredibly, many embezzlers live under the deception that they somehow have a right to do this. They come to see the other person's wealth as their own.

God owns everything, including the homes, possessions, and money that we hold in trust for Him. He graciously gives us up to 90 percent of what we hold to use for saving, investing, and spending. He expects at least 10 percent of that trust to be returned to His store-house—the local church and ministries that flow from it. This tithe is to be taken off the top—the firstfruits. When we divert that tithe from His intended purpose (giving) into our pockets (saving, investing, spending), we embezzle from Him. We rob God.

In the case of Achan, the secret sin of one man dramatically affected many people and the momentum of the movement of God. I've often wondered, "Does the secret sin of embezzling God's resources by not tithing, especially if the individual is a leader, have the potential to affect a congregation's momentum?" If the answer is yes, it's no wonder many churches are impotent, for there is an epidemic of embezzling among Christians in our materialistic culture!

REVERSING MOMENTUM

Disobedience caused by deception is the quickest way to lose or reverse momentum. That's true both personally and organizationally. Achan may have convinced himself that secret sin doesn't matter— what they don't know won't hurt them. Secret sin, however, has public consequences. The God who was with Israel (6:27) now allowed His anger to burn against them (7:1).

Disobedience by one led to the defeat of all. This defeat brought not only physical loss (death) but also emotional and spiritual loss as "the hearts of the people melted" (7:5). Earlier, when the spies were scouting the land, Rahab had described that same fear running through Israel's enemies. She said, "Our hearts melted and everyone's courage failed because of you" (2:11). What had been true of their enemies was now true of them. This was a momentum meltdown. Just

as small acts of obedience build momentum, so small acts of disobedience stall it. Achan's disobedience resulted in a loss of confidence
that permeated the whole nation of Israel. It can happen to whole
congregations too.

RECOGNIZING THE PROBLEM

Joshua, the leader, was unaware of Achan's sin. God sometimes
slow things down—or even grinds them to a halt—so leaders can
become aware of beneath-the-surface issues. When things are moving
quickly, leaders tend to hydroplane. Downshifting may be necessary
in order to recognize and deal with deceptions that have taken place.

Joshua responded to the devastating situation with actions that
showed deep humility. He tore his clothes, fell face down before ark,
and remained in God's presence rather than rushing out to fix the
problem (7:6). The other leaders of Israel did the same, adding to
their expression of regret by sprinkling dust on their heads.

Joshua prayed, asking the question that was on everyone's mind,
"Ah, Sovereign LORD, why? . . ." (7:7–9). Simultaneously submitting
to God's sovereignty and asking the "why" question is the key to
receiving revelation. While Joshua's prayer starts strong, and will end
strong, his confusion is evident. Let's trace his emotions in this prayer.

First, Joshua blamed God. His question assumed that God's leadership is the source of the problem. "Why did You ever bring this
people across the Jordan to deliver us into the hands of the Amorites
to destroy us?"

Next, he lost vision. Joshua even wished the Israelites had never
moved forward in the first place. "If we had only been content to stay
on the other side of the Jordan." In this case, Joshua's feigned contentment with the previous situation is a cover for a lack of faith. In despair
he is succumbed to the danger of the "if only" syndrome. His mis-
placed regret for crossing the Jordan is not a substitute for repentance.

Then he became selfish. Joshua's self-centered concern is for
what he can say about the predicament (7:8) and for what the enemy

will do to them (7:9). That's where many super-responsible people begin their prayers—with what they can say about the situation.

Joshua's honest prayer, like the prayers of many struggling spiritual leaders, focused more on himself than on God. It reflects a certain double-mindedness. Eventually, however, Joshua moves beyond self-absorption to concern for God's reputation. "What then will you do for you own great name" (7:9)? Spiritual leaders must rise above their concern for the management of a crisis. Their ultimate concern must be for the potential impact of the situation upon God's reputation.

God's answer (7:10–12) confirms that Joshua's constructive humility (7:6) had degenerated into destructive self-pity (7:10). There are times to kneel down and times to take a stand. This was a time to "stand up!" Let's follow God's response to Joshua.

First, God revealed the area of disobedience and deception (7:11). Israel had violated the covenant God had told them to keep. They had stolen from God by taking devoted things as their own possessions. They had lied.

Then God revealed the reason for their defeat. "That is why . . ." (7:12). God gave a direct answer to Joshua's earlier "why" question (7:7). Disobedience and deception result in defeat and destruction (7:11–12).

Finally, God distanced Himself from His people, but let it be known that this distance could be overcome by deeds of repentance (7:12). Joshua's original commission had been accompanied by a promise: "As I was with Moses, so I will be with you. I will never leave you or forsake you" (1:5). Now Joshua was reminded of the condition of this promise: obedience. "I will not be with you anymore unless. . . ."

This is the downward spiral of deception seen in so many leaders and churches.

DOWNWARD SPIRAL OF DECEPTION

Tragically, many leaders continue to try moving forward without the empowering presence of God. Where there is defeat, God says that we need to go back to where it all began. We need to return to the root of the problem—disobedience and deception.

SEEKING GOD

To deal with deception one must confront the truth. God forced Israel to do that after the devastating defeat at Ai. Just as God had involved all the people in the victory of Jericho, so He involves everyone in dealing with deception. The steps He led Israel through then are similar to the steps He now uses to lead His people in replacing deception with devotion.

Consecration (7:13). First, God instructed the people to consecrate themselves to Him. This ritual of purification was the necessary preparation for meeting with God. When the people stood before their holy God, they had to be holy people. There would be no revelation from God until His people were first consecrated to Him.

While we no longer use rituals of purification, we, too, must be consecrated to God if He is to speak to us. He wants to know that we are ready to be both "hearers and doers" of what He will communicate to us.

Presentation (7:14–18). Next, God set a time—the next morning when the people would present themselves to Him. Imagine the suspense they must have felt. Undoubtedly they missed a good night's sleep! They would present themselves to God tribe by tribe, clan by clan, family by family, man by man. God has stipulated a process that would reveal the exact source of the deception. Joshua began leading them through this process early (7:16) the next morning. I'm sure the people were up already!

What would be an equivalent process for a church that wanted to discover why God was distant from them? Notice that God led His people through a process that moved from general to specific. Like peeling back the layers of an onion, He brought them to the core of the issue. A church might approximate that by conducting a self-analysis that examined department by department, ministry by ministry, class by class, group by group. How courageous it would be for a church to undertake a time of congregational soul searching in order to discover the reasons they were not experiencing spiritual victory.

UNCOVERING CAUSES OF DECEPTION IN CHURCHES

Congregational self-deception is a cancer that first spreads and then kills churches. In many churches the search for new ideas and tools to create church health is a way of avoiding the problem. What are some common causes of deception?

Abuse of Power. Pastors or lay persons may become consumed with personal power. They naïvely view a "my way or the highway" approach to conflict resolution as evidence of strong leadership. They blindly believe that their personal agenda is God's plan for ministry. The abuser of power divides the fellowship and restricts vision yet imagines others as the cause of the problem.

Lack of Accountability. When a head-in-the-sand approach to leadership is substituted for speaking the truth in love, there are many possible deceptions. Money may be spent in ways it shouldn't be. A relationship that has become emotionally or physically inappropriate may be allowed to continue. Personal and organizational discipline may be sacrificed as promises are broken and important questions are left unasked and unanswered.

Legalism. Legalism is the introduction of new standards of spirituality that go beyond the clear teaching of Scripture. This problem is as old as Eve, who falsely quoted God as saying they weren't to touch the tree at the center of the Garden. God had said only that they were not to eat from it. Legalism begets false pride in adhering to one's own criteria for spirituality—usually a list of do's and don'ts—rather than the humility that comes from obeying God's simple commands.

Lukewarmness. Lukewarmness occurs when people are blinded to their true spiritual needs and exercise a faith devoid of repentance. In lukewarm churches, the call to holiness falls on deaf ears, if it is issued at all. The church becomes nothing more than a social club.

Cynicism. Cynicism is an attitude that condemns new or different ideas without consideration. Cynics imagine themselves as defenders of tradition or discerners of true spirituality, but the hallmark of their Christianity is criticism rather than love. That critical spirit repels new people and new ideas, leaving the cynic with the smug impression that he has honored God.

UNCOVERING CAUSES OF DECEPTION IN OURSELVES

Deception is equally cancerous in the life of a leader. We must engage in a regular and relentless process of identifying self-deception and breaking free from it. If God seems distant and spiritual defeat is prevalent, a leader should ask soul-searching questions in these areas.

Physical. Am I a good steward of my body, God's temple? Do I lack self-control so that I am driven by fleshly desires?

Mental. Are my thoughts centered on what is excellent and praiseworthy? Are my attitudes like those of Christ Jesus in every arena of my life?

Emotional. Do my feelings follow my faith or lead it? Are my emotions appropriately expressed to God and others?

Financial. Do I rob God? Am I in bondage to debt or addicted to spending? Do I find security in my savings and investments rather than in God?

Relational. Do I speak the truth in love? Is there an unresolved conflict or root of bitterness in my life?

Spiritual. Do I daily quiet my heart to experience intimacy with God? Do I respond to His Spirit's prompting in my life?

I make it a daily practice to parade each arena of my life before God in prayer so He can specifically reveal any self-deception.

Yet I can easily fool myself. I must never assume that I will automatically see my weaknesses. That's the nature of self-deception, after all. The Apostle Paul had a healthy suspicion of his own conscience. "My conscience is clear, but that does not make me innocent. It is the Lord who judges me" (1 Cor. 4:4).

Frankly, I don't always trust myself to answer these self-accountability questions honestly. So I periodically have others examine my life, namely my spouse, my accountability partner, staff members, and church board members. I've seen many colleagues fail morally at times when they perceived themselves to be spiritually strong. I've heard leaders I love excuse ongoing sins of gluttony, greed, anger, and selfishness. When they continue to live with self-deception, the power of their personal example dies a slow death.

REMOVING SELF-DECEPTION

Self-deception by either a church or leader is debilitating, but it need not be fatal. Once deception has been identified, it can be dealt with. Here are the steps that God used in moving Israel out of self-deception into the power of truth.

Confession (7:19–23). When all the people had presented themselves, the searchlight fell upon Achan. Interestingly, Joshua didn't respond with anger but addressed Achan in a fatherly fashion—"My son." He encouraged Achan to glorify God by revealing what he had done. God receives praise when that which is hidden comes to light.

Achan's confession ("It is true!") included a statement of both his sinful action ("This is what I have done") and the attitude that fueled it ("I coveted").

Most Christians probably think of making music as the primary way in which they praise God. Many of our musical offerings, in fact, are labeled "praise songs." But shouldn't we also offer the praise of confession to God? God is glorified when disobedience is acknowledged and fresh surrender is made to Him.

Devotion (7:24–26). After Achan confessed, that which was supposed to be devoted to the Lord was finally given to Him. Tragically, the consequences of Achan's secret sin had a very public impact on those he loved. His deception cost not only his life but also the lives of his family members as well as thirty-six soldiers (7:5). The Lord brought disaster on the one who brought disaster upon His people.

Later repentance never substitutes for earlier obedience. It's always best to experience God's preventing power to keep us from sin rather than His intervening power to cleanse us from sin. That cleansing will purify our hearts but will not nullify the consequences of our actions.

In Israel's case, "the LORD turned from His fierce anger" (7:26). Many churches need to experience a turnaround. I wonder how many of those turnarounds might begin if leaders took the actions that would cause God to turn from His anger.

EXPERIENCING RESTORATION

Once the people of Israel completed the steps that removed deception—consecration, presentation, confession, and devotion—God restored them. The record of this restoration is found in Joshua, chapter 8.

Encouragement. Their restoration began with a rekindling of courage—"Do not be afraid; do not be discouraged" (8:1). This same call was given to Joshua as he began his leadership role (1:9) and would be repeated later in the face of other leadership challenges (10:25). God knows that if leaders remain discouraged their failures will be final.

Sermon Potential

The Bible mentions about four hundred leaders. Only about eighty finish well. Robert Clinton, a leading thinker in the area of Christian leadership, estimates that 70 percent of today's Christian leaders don't finish well. This doesn't mean that they fail morally but that their influence wanes rather than waxes as their ministries progress. They stop being teachable. They neglect the disciplines that develop character. They stop living by their convictions. Their relationship with God grows distant. They lose the sense of wonder about working for God. Dan Webster, in his *Leadership of the Heart* seminar, attributes this tendency to finish poorly to three pitfalls. The first is laziness. The second is sin. The third, and perhaps the most common, is discouragement.

Discouragement usually affects us in areas where we've once been defeated. Since Israel had been defeated by Ai, the thought of attacking them again was discouraging. So God diverted their attention from that defeat to an earlier victory—"You shall do to Ai and its kings as you did to Jericho and its king" (8:2). God also noted a distinction between Ai and Jericho. Since Jericho was the first city conquered, the plunder was considered firstfruits and was to be completely devoted to God. Now that they had fulfilled that commitment by exposing Achan's sin and devoting the stolen articles, the plunder Ai would be theirs to keep.

By God's grace, Israel's previous defeat became a platform for victory (8:2–7). They attacked the city again, this time planning to draw the men of Ai into an ambush. The plan worked as the shameful retreat which was the evidence of their earlier loss (7:5) became a strategy for luring the army of Ai away from the protection of the city (8:6). When weaknesses are turned to strengths it is evidence that God is at work.

Realignment. God's restoration of Israel resulted in a complete realignment of their faith. One evidence of that is the realignment of God's commands and Joshua's orders (8:8). God gave the mandate, and Joshua translated it into specific action. Deception leads us to question God's faithfulness; restoration brings renewed faith in the Lord's commands and an eagerness to obey.

Also, following Israel's defeat of Ai, Joshua led the people in worship (8:30–35). A service of worship can be the capstone for a restoration process. Joshua built an altar to make offerings and had the Law of Moses copied onto stones. He positioned the people around the ark and had every word of the law of Moses read to them, including the promise of blessings for obedience and curses for disobedience. While we no longer build altars or carve stones, we can testify to our renewed relationship with God by offering our worship to Him and by learning from His Word.

DECEPTION FROM THE OUTSIDE: LACK OF DISCERNMENT

There is a second origin of deception. In the case of Achan, it came from inside the camp and began with the disobedience of God's people. It was self-deception, deception from within. Deception can also come from without. Joshua, chapter 9, tells the story of Israel's deception by the Gibeonites, a Canaanite people who tricked Israel into making a treaty with them. This episode did not begin with disobedience but resulted in it. The two situations may be contrasted this way:

DECEPTION FROM THE INSIDE Achan: Joshua 7	DECEPTION FROM THE OUTSIDE The Gibeonites: Joshua 9
Disobedience and Deception (7:1)	Deception (9:1–13)
Defeat and Destruction (7:2–5)	Disobedience (9:14–15)
Distance from God (7:6–12)	Disunity (9:16–21)

No matter what the source, deception debilitates God's people and inhibits their forward progress. Joshua's failure to respond prayerfully and carefully to the Gibeonite's offer resulted in deception rather than discernment.

For spiritual leaders, deception is a constant threat. Our ultimate enemy, Satan, is a deceiver by nature. His first interaction with the human race was an attempt to deceive Eve. His last interaction with the human race will be an attempt to deceive the nations (Rev. 20:7–8). So we must constantly be on guard against not only self-deception but also the deceptions of Satan.

To do that, we need discernment. We may gain that by understanding how the Gibeonites fooled Joshua and the leaders of Israel. Their failure to discern the truth provides a chilling lesson for us.

THE CORRUPTION OF DISCERNMENT

Discerning leaders are not deceived. Therefore the first step in the deception of a leader is the corruption of his or her discernment. This insidious process has resulted in disobedience by more Christian leaders than we would care to remember. Here's how that process progressed with the leaders of Israel.

There Was an Emphasis on Appearance (9:3–6). The Gibeonites prepared an elaborate ruse by loading their donkeys with worn-out sacks and wineskins, wearing worn and patched clothing and sandals, and bringing a food supply of dry and moldy bread. That made it appear that they had come from a great distance, well beyond the boundary that God had established as the forbidden zone for peace treaties.

False appearance is the essence of deception. Satan masquerades as an angel of light, a wolf in sheep's clothing. Leaders must look beneath the surface. While we must not succumb to cynicism, neither can we be naïve. We must recognize there are two sides to every story and seek out both sides. Discernment means doing some digging.

They Were Easily Dissuaded from Their Initial Concerns (9:7–8). To their credit, the leaders of Israel were suspicious of the story they were told. Leaders often have a certain intuition about communication that doesn't quite ring true. They need to listen to that intuition. This would have been a great place for Israel's leaders to take a time-out and prayerfully process those concerns. That would have moved their suspicions from the level of personal intuition to spiritual discernment.

Business writer Jim Collins discovered that the ability to practice disciplined thought is a trait of great companies. He describes this as the "discipline to confront the brutal facts of reality while retaining the resolute faith that you can and will create a path to greatness."[1] Faith does not ignore concerns. Rather, it fully investigates concerns without losing its focus on God.

This ability to confront reality is also a characteristic of good relationships among leaders. Greg Hawkins, executive pastor of Willow Creek Community Church in Illinois, has a productive relationship with senior pastor Bill Hybels. Hawkins says, "I can always count on Bill to say the tough things, to address the tough issues. I never have to wonder about what he is thinking. If he has something to say to me, he says it."[2]

It would be speculation to say that some of the leaders of Israel had stronger suspicions than others, but that is often the case when an organization faces the need for discernment. Those with the strongest suspicions must calmly and convincingly express them to the group. Those who don't share those suspicions need to listen carefully and openly to the concerns of others. Fully processing concerns is a mark of strength in a leadership team.

They Were Flattered by the Offer They Received (9:8–9, 11). When the Israelite leaders raised questions about the Gibeonites, they answered evasively at first, saying only, "We are your servants." Since their ancestors had suffered as slaves in Egypt for so many years, the idea of having servants must have been flattering to the Israelites. That flattery opened the door to further deception.

Pride is the enemy of discernment and the ally of deception. Flattery inflates the ego. The flatterer's compliments make him appear to be gracious, and it's difficult to ask tough questions of an apparently benevolent person. Joshua would have been wise to recognize that this offer had nothing to do with God's promise of land. The Israelites were never promised that they would have servants from far-off countries. Flattery may lead us to seek perks that God never included in His covenant with us.

A flattering offer should raise a red flag. It should motivate us to look carefully at the intentions of the person making the offer and the obligations we might incur on accepting it.

They Were Misled by the Spiritualization of the Situation (9:9–10). The Gibeonites furthered their deception by spiritualizing the situation. They indicated that their long journey had been motivated by "the fame of the LORD your God." Then they recounted the past victories God had provided for Israel against the Egyptians and the Amorites. Deception often is wrapped in a most spiritual sounding package.

Spiritualizing is the effort to bolster a weak argument with religious language. It's baptizing a selfish desire with the words "God told me." It's saying "God's not present in our worship services like He used to be" when the real issue is the personal preference of music style. It's purporting that the church has "lost its sense of warmth and fellowship" when the problem is really a loss of personal attention. Deceivers often use spiritualization to mask self-interest.

They Were Misled by Their Senses (9:8–14). Deception is most powerful when it involves all the senses. The Israelites began to be deceived by what they *heard* (8–11). The deception was reinforced by what they *saw* (12–13). It even included their sense of *taste* (14). When physical senses become a substitute for spiritual senses, deception is certain.

Good
Devo

Discernment is based on spiritual senses. Repeatedly the Bible calls us to have spiritual "eyes that see" and "ears that hear." The mark of a spiritually mature leader is the ability to grasp truths which can be discerned only spiritually. That requires the mind of Christ (1 Cor. 2:14–16).

They Failed to Pray Before Making a Significant Decision (9:14–15). The Israelite leaders "did not inquire of the LORD" about the Gibeonites' treaty offer. Presumption replaced prayer. If Joshua had sought God in prayer, He would have been warned of the deception. If Joshua had led the other leaders in a prayer meeting, certainly they too would have sensed that something was amiss.

Israel's disobedience deepened as they entered a treaty of peace with the Gibeonites and ratified it with an oath. Human alliance replaced dependence upon God. God had repeatedly warned His people against forming alliances with neighboring nations. He alone would deliver Israel. Sometimes making peace leads to a compromise that is nothing more than disobedience.

They Rushed Their Decision (9:16). Three days later, the Israelites received word that the Gibeonites were not distant travelers but nearby neighbors. Three days! What if Joshua had simply allowed a little time to pass before acting? A delay of just three days would have brought the truth to light.

Sometimes delaying a decision for even a short time makes all the difference. One of the reasons God sometimes moves slowly is to allow time for His people to discern what's really happening. Moving quickly increases the possibility of deception. There are rare occasions when quick action is warranted. More often, quick action is a substitute for careful preparation.

THE CONSEQUENCES OF DECEPTION

The Israelites eventually discovered that they had been deceived, but the consequences of their hasty action were already set. Deception from without is often uncovered very easily. The damage, however, may not always be undone. Here's the aftermath of Israel's failure to discern.

Their Disobedience Brought Disunity (9:15–21). Making peace with the Gibeonites (15) brought dissension among the Israelites (18). The whole assembly grumbled upon hearing that their leaders had struck an improper alliance. When leaders compromise by placating one faction inappropriately, they generally lose the support of faithful people.

Many churches have been divided by leaders who cater to various groups, trying to "maintain peace and unity." Rather than leading with prayerful conviction, they become increasingly frenzied in their effort to meet competing demands.

Their Promises, Though Based on Deception, Had to Be Kept (9:19–27). Because the Israelites had ratified their treaty with an oath to God, they had to honor it, even though it was made under false pretenses. The leaders of Israel rightly insisted that they must live by their word. In fact, later in Israel's history the failure to keep this promise resulted in a famine (2 Sam. 21:1, 4, 6). In this case, a deal was a deal.

Part of what makes deception so painful is that its consequences remain long after the lesson has been learned. If not careful, a leader who discovers that he has been deceived may resort to a victim mentality. I know some leaders who seem to focus only on what others have done to harm them, even in small ways. Generally, they ignore the role that they played in creating the situation, insisting that "it's all their fault." A victim mentality leads to bitterness and paralyzes us in the past. A vision mentality, one focused on what we can learn and change, propels us into a brighter future.

Churches as well as individuals can develop a victim mentality. I know of a church that has been hurt by the deceptive actions of a previous pastor. That pastor was wrong and has gone through a process of restoration. Yet the church continues to replay the pain of the past rather than learn what it can from that difficult experience and move on. The present pastor finds it impossible to communicate a vision for the future to this church that sees itself as a victim of the past.

Whatever destruction has been wrought in our lives by deception—either deception by self or deception by others—we must ask God to bring the necessary healing, learn the important lessons, and then allow the vision of a glorious future to emerge.

PERSONAL REFLECTION

1. Can you think of a time when you deceived yourself, only later to see things as they truly were? What eventually helped you to "see the light"?

2. What safeguards have you built into your life to protect against self-deception? Who have you empowered to ask tough questions of you?

3. Have you ever been deceived by others? How did you feel? What did you do to move beyond the deception?

4. Review the self-evaluation questions in the section titled "Uncovering Causes of Deception in Ourselves," and search for self-deception in your physical, mental, emotional, financial, relational, and spiritual life.

INVENTORY FOR SPIRITUAL LEADERS

1. Joshua's prayer in Josh. 7:6–9 reflects some common weaknesses of leaders. In what way do you see those weaknesses in your own leadership?

   - *Joshua blamed God.* Is there any failure for which you blame God?
   - *Joshua lost vision.* Have you lost the vision for any area of your ministry?
   - *Joshua became selfish.* Is there some area of ministry that has become "all about you" rather than about serving God and others?

2. Review the common areas of deception for churches. Do any apply to your church or area of ministry?

3. Why do you think so many spiritual leaders fail to finish well? What is most likely to trip you up and keep you from finishing well?

4. The leaders of Israel failed to pray before making a significant commitment. In what ways does prayer increase a leader's discernment? When you're about to make a big commitment, what should you include in your prayer for discernment?

5. Some churches and ministries develop a victim mentality, living in the pain of the past rather than entering the future God has for them. What consequences of adopting a victim mentality have you seen in others or in yourself? How can a leader or church avoid that trap?

JOSHUA'S JOURNAL

Lord, I recognize that it's easy to be deceived by others, easier to be deceived by myself. Please bring to light any ways in which I'm fooling myself. Help me to be open to the godly counsel of others whom You may be sending to warn me. Lord, please help me to "see the light" before the consequences of deception significantly affect my relationship with You and my ministry to others. Amen.

CHAPTER SIX

MAINTAINING

MOMENTUM

—⟋⟋⟍—

STALL FACTOR: Personal limitations.

FORWARD STEP: Do not allow your skills to confine God's mission.

I was emotionally drained. We had just buried my friend, my hero, my mentor—my father. Sixty years of age seemed far too young for him to die. His death left me feeling empty, and the vacuum was expanded by my disappointment that God had not healed him. It required my total energy to fulfill the most basic responsibilities to my family and ministry.

Dad's death occurred at a time when our congregation was poised to take a huge step of faith. After years of cramming worshippers into an inadequately-sized multipurpose building four or five times each weekend, we were set to build our new Celebration Center. The financial commitment was daunting, and a strong leader

Trust is the lubrication which makes it possible for organizations to work.

—Warren Bennis

You then, my son, be strong in the grace that is in Christ Jesus. And the things you have heard me say in the presence of many witnesses entrust to reliable men who will also be qualified to teach others.

—2 Timothy 2:1–2

was needed to give the people both reassurance and confidence.

My grief and my responsibilities as a leader collided at this pivotal point in my ministry. Would I take time out for personal recovery and perhaps miss a window of opportunity for construction of the Celebration Center? Or would I push ahead at who knew what risk to my spiritual and emotional health? Or was there a third possibility? Was it possible that these two realities were being used by God to create another option that was not yet apparent?

There are pivotal points in every leader's life. If successfully navigated, they result in personal growth and ministry expansion. But if the leader gets stuck at one of these hurdles, it places an artificial boundary on both his personal development and ministry.

JOSHUA'S TURNING POINT

Shiloh

The middle chapters of the book of Joshua seem at first to contain merely a routine record of the conquest of certain areas within the Promised Land and a listing of the inheritance for each tribe of Israel. But buried among these lists of places and names are the pivotal points in Joshua's life. None is more important than the one found in Josh. 13:1. "When Joshua was old and well advanced in years, the LORD said to him, 'You are very old, and there are still very large areas of land to be taken.'"

Two realities collided in Joshua's life: his personal limitations and the scope of the remaining mission. The Lord pointed out to him the pivotal point that would redefine his ministry and shape the remainder of his life.

THE REALITY OF PERSONAL LIMITATIONS

The first reality is Joshua's personal limitations: "You are very old." Estimates place his age at this point at ninety to one hundred years. Joshua's limitation is physical—age is catching up with him. With the advance of years come certain limitations. Several years ago Jim Buick, then CEO of Zondervan Corporation, spoke to a leadership luncheon at our church. He had recently announced his retirement from Zondervan, which came in the midst of a reorganization that he had engineered. In the question and answer time following his presentation, he was asked what was next for him. He commented that he would be more of a mentor than a leader in the next season of his life because "generals don't go to war in the twilight of their lives." Jim was acknowledging the limits of age yet remaining engaged in a ministry fitting for his life stage.

Everyone faces personal limitations; age is only one of them. One of the most perplexing for me personally is a limited energy level. While I have bursts of energy for starting new endeavors, my overall battery is lower than that of most leaders with similar responsibilities. Many times I've asked God to raise my energy level, to help me get by on less than the eight hours of sleep I seem to require each night. He has left that limit in place.

The Apostle Paul had a personal limitation, which he called a "thorn in the flesh" (2 Cor. 12:7–10). While we don't know the exact nature of this limitation, we do know that Paul asked that it be removed—three times! The thorn remained, but his anxiety about it was replaced by confidence in God's grace to endure. Paul came to believe that this weakness would allow God's strength to develop in his life. The personal limitation would be used for God's glory.

Leaders encounter many personal limitations:

- Age.

- Physical diseases or disability.

- Diminishing mental capacities.

- Special needs of family members.

- Lack of resources, money, or energy.

- Limited spiritual gifts or leadership skills.

In some cases, the effect of a personal limitation can be minimized or mitigated, but only rarely eliminated. I can raise my energy level by eating right and sleeping well. I can manage it by pacing myself and setting clear priorities. Even so, I can only progress so far before I reach biological boundaries.

An unhealthy response to the reality of a personal limitations is denial. Denial creates a blind spot, causing the leader to conclude that everything is fine. Those that follow that leader usually know better, and the leader's denial erodes his or her credibility. Denial only deepens the impact of the limitation because a limitation must be acknowledged in order to be managed.

THE REALITY OF THE UNFULFILLED MISSION

The second reality Joshua had to face was the scope of the mission yet to be fulfilled: "There are still very large areas of land to be taken." In the verses that follow God specified the regions that remained unconquered and the enemies who dwelled in them. The list must have left an aging Joshua feeling overwhelmed.

An unhealthy response to the reality of a vast remaining mission is to downsize the mission to fit within the leader's limited reach. Many churches are not growing while multitudes of people in the community around them are heading toward a Christless eternity. The reason is not lack of facilities, money, or volunteers—though these may be the stated reasons. The real reason is that the leaders have put a lid on the mission so that they won't have to face their personal limitations. The God-sized vision entrusted to them is reduced to fit comfortably within their man-sized limitations.

Those two realities beg this question of Joshua: What will you do about the vast remaining mission in light of your increasing personal limitations?

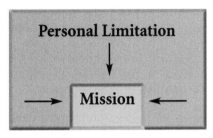

Most leaders don't face this dilemma only once. As I look back over my own life, I can identify at least a few such turning points. During these times of transition, God moves slowly to help the leader understand the reality of the situation and respond in a way that results in personal growth and ministry expansion.

Notice that God did not limit the mission to conform to Joshua's personal limitations (13:6–7). Instead, God reaffirmed His commitment to give Israel the whole Promised Land—"I myself will drive them out before the Israelites." Then He asked Joshua to change his approach to leadership—"Be sure to allocate this land to Israel for an inheritance, as I have instructed you. . . ."

Now Joshua could have reached this pivotal point and concluded it was time for him to retire. It would have been easy to see his encroaching age as the end of his leadership. Or perhaps Joshua considered changing roles and finding a challenge more in keeping with the abilities of an older man.

That's a choice made by many leaders who feel personal limitations placing a lid on their leadership ability. My first reaction when feeling my limits is to wonder whether it's time for me to move. At times it is appropriate to change one's role or to fulfill the same role in a smaller setting. But often, God is not calling a limited leader to a new role but to a new responsibility within our current role. He's not calling the leader to go but to grow.

Joshua rightly saw this pivotal moment as a call to a new way of leading. Perhaps what God called Joshua to do is exactly what He wants most leaders to do at the pivotal points in their ministries— define, delegate, and develop. A leader defines the contribution he or she must make, delegates the achievement of the mission to other leaders, then develops them to successfully fulfill their roles.

DEFINING YOUR ROLE

Everyday I pause for a moment during my quiet time with God to lay my calling before Him. As I mentioned earlier, I ask Him for three things related to my calling—clarity, intensity, and tenacity. That first request, for greater clarity, acknowledges my tendency to allow my sense of calling to get fuzzy. An ill-focused calling leads to diffusion of energy and loss of impact.

Most of us who serve as spiritual leaders find ourselves in an odd situation. We have been taught how to minister to others but not how to build our own ministries. We can counsel other people but can't clarify our own unique contribution. We can deliver a message to others but falter in giving direction to ourselves. This is a common situation and one we can manage with prayer and planning.

If we don't seek God for the design of our own ministries, we are left to duplicate the ministry of someone else. This rarely works because God has given each of us different passions, gifts, and personalities. We end up trying to be someone we are not. Like David, who realized that King Saul's armor was ill-fitting and inappropriate for his mission to slay Goliath (1 Sam. 17:38–40), we, too, must understand ourselves and the ways that God has gifted us to lead.

We R Unique

Here are some questions that have led to the clarification of my calling.

MINISTER VERSUS EQUIPPER

Am I a minister or an equipper? A minister is primarily a doer of ministry, someone who uses personal gifts to touch the lives of others.

Ministers act directly—they preach sermons, give counsel, teach classes, make calls, and delight in being on the front lines with people. They relate readily to Paul's charge to Timothy:

> Preach the Word; be prepared in season and out of season; correct, rebuke, and encourage—with great patience and careful instruction. . . . keep your head in all situations, endure hardship, do the work of an evangelist, discharge all the duties of your ministry (2 Tim. 4:2, 5).

An equipper, on the other hand, is primarily a developer of other people and their gifts. Equippers minister indirectly—they prepare others to serve on the front lines of ministry. While they likely engage is some preaching or teaching, their first love is to develop others who have gifts in teaching, exhortation, and prophecy. Rather than making many calls themselves, they raise up a team of caregivers. Equippers often quote Eph. 4:11–12:

> It was he who gave some to be apostles, some to be prophets, some to be evangelists, and some to be pastors and teachers, to prepare God's people for works of service, so that the body of Christ may be built up. . . .

Is one right and the other wrong? One biblical and the other not? No! We each must understand who we are and then find a ministry setting that's conducive to living out that calling. Both ministers and equippers are used by God to build healthy churches. It is tragic that ministers sometimes disparage equippers—they label them as CEOs, saying that they are "simply running a business." It's equally damaging when equippers take a condescending attitude toward ministers. That attitude is prevalent in the current ministry culture, where pastors who are doers at heart have felt marginalized and pressured to adopt the *rancher* approach to ministry.

Ministering and equipping are not exclusive of one another. Every equipper should continue some involvement in direct ministry. Every minister should equip others to do some of the work of the ministry.

Each pastor needs to assess his or her passions, gifts, and temperament to determine which approach primarily characterizes his or her ministry.

As a rule of thumb, ministers are most effective in churches under three hundred, where most of their schedule is filled with preaching, counseling, and calling. They tend to struggle when the congregation grows to the point that they can't keep up with the demands. Equippers tend to be more effective in larger churches, where parishioners more readily recognize that it is impossible for them to do most of the ministry and expect that it will be done through others. Equippers tend to struggle in settings where the majority of their ministry calls for one-to-one pastoral skills.

Someone who serves well as a minister may well face this pivotal question—as I produce fruit in ministry and gain greater responsibility, will I move to a setting that allows me to continue serving as a minister or will I become an equipper? Ministers who effectively preach God's Word and reach out to people through counseling, calling, and evangelism will likely see growth in their churches. They may be called to a church when it averages one hundred in attendance, and their faithful ministry may build it to three hundred. At that point, an equipper may be needed in order to produce continued growth. The pastor's dilemma: Should I become that equipper or should I go to another church of one hundred and build it up?

When identifying your primary approach to ministry, be sure that you don't have preconceived ideas about these roles. I attend a small group along with a pastor I admire greatly. He has faithfully led a congregation for many years, leading it from a dysfunctional church on the brink of closure to a healthy congregation poised to break the two hundred barrier. He is highly relational and loves investing time in people. Somehow he was given the impression that in order to lead the church beyond two hundred he would have to suppress his desire to relate to people and become primarily an administrator. In reality, he may simply need to focus his relational bent more intentionally on developing lay ministers who can then meet the needs of others. That would create a relational ripple that moved from him to other leaders to the congregation as a whole.

The next step for this pastor was not to become something he wasn't but to refine his greatest strength to accomplish a wider goal.

Which are you primarily? _____Minister __X__Equipper

LBA Structure _____

To Do versus to Delegate

What are the essential responsibilities I must fulfill and may not delegate to others? There are two steps to answering this question. One is to examine each responsibility to determine whether it should be done in the first place. As Peter Drucker says, "Nothing is less productive than to make more efficient what should not be done at all."[1] So in order to answer this question, we must assess the present-day validity of our activities. It may be that a "not to do" list is more important than a "to do" list.

The second step in answering this question is to determine whether I am the one who should do the thing that should be done. Could others do it? Should others do it? When our church was formed, there were many things that needed to be done, and I was the one who needed to do them. As the church has increased the quality and quantity of its ministries, I have done fewer and fewer things. Now, there are only three things that the board and I have identified as essential to my ministry as senior pastor—worship leadership, vision casting, and leadership development.

This question moves us from the assumption that everything is ministry to the discernment of the essential things in ministry. List the activities that currently fill your calendar. Identify the items that are essential and must be done. Identify which of these essentials you must not delegate and must do yourself:

ACTIVITY	MUST BE DONE?	MUST BE DONE BY ME?
Meetings,		X
Leadership		X
Lesson Prep	Dave X Me	
Paper Stuff	Janet X Gwen	
Personal Growth	X	

TO ACCEPT VERSUS TO DECLINE

What must I say no to? It may be possible to accomplish anything we truly want in life, but it is impossible to accomplish everything. Successful leaders have learned to say no to opportunities that do not contribute to the mission to which God has called them.

The Apostle Paul regularly left churches that loved him and would have welcomed his leadership for years to come. On one occasion we're given a glimpse of the pain a church felt at his parting. "They all wept as they embraced him and kissed him. What grieved them most was his statement that they would never see his face again . . ." (Acts 20:37–38).

Why would Paul say no to the opportunity to remain in leadership at a church that loved him and where there was so much yet to be done? Because his calling lay elsewhere. Romans 15:20 reveals Paul's mission: "It has always been my ambition to preach the gospel where Christ was not known, so that I would not be building on someone else's foundation." Paul was always moving on to the next city where a church planting project was needed.

One of the pastors I greatly admire is a church planter named Wayne Otto. Wayne planted a church in Greenville, Michigan, and led it to become a thriving congregation that has greatly influenced that community. Under Wayne's leadership, the congregation grew to several hundred people, and there was tremendous potential for future growth. Yet he felt called to leave and start all over again in a nearby community, Ionia. The church in Ionia was no sooner launched when Wayne began dreaming of the next place where God will lead him. Do the churches in Greenville and Ionia have many good years ahead of them? Certainly. But by leaving, Wayne is saying no to something good in order to honor the calling God has placed upon his life.

When the choice is between good and bad, little discernment is required. When the choice is between better and best, we must pray so that we "may be able to discern what is best" (Phil. 1:10). Saying no clarifies a vision more than saying yes. When you put your yes's and no's together, your sense of calling will be crystal clear.

List the opportunities that are currently before you. Rank them with 1 being best, 2 second best, and so on.

OPPORTUNITY	RANK
Assistant Pastor	4
Staff Pastor	2
Youth Pastor	3
Senior Pastor	1
Church Planter	5
Blue Collar Worker	6

TRACKING GOD'S LEADING

Do I keep track of the occasions when God's Spirit has prompted me? I make entries into my journal on a daily basis. I record what I sense are God's promptings for my personal life, relationships, and pastoral leadership. The simple act of writing them down solidifies some of God's messages to me. Reading over them later usually reveals themes that bring longer-term definition to my roles as a follower of Christ, husband, father, friend, and pastor.

"It's been estimated that 97 percent of business people do not set goals. Of this group, entrepreneurs are above average—more than 80 percent spend no time each day setting goals or planning, 15 percent spend up to 12 minutes, and only 5 percent spend at least 15 minutes a day planning for themselves."[2] That means that while they work hard and long, their efforts are often unfocused and unproductive. What a loss!

But there is a greater loss, which has eternal consequences. It's the failure of spiritual leaders to take time each day to ask God what He wants to say and do through them. What would the percentages be? Could it be said that 80 percent of Christian leaders spend no time each day praying for and mapping the leading of God's Spirit? This failure, repeated day after day, causes leaders to drift from God's design. It also confirms the reality so clearly communicated by Jesus: "If you remain in me and I in you, you will bear much fruit; apart from me you can do nothing" (John 15:5).

I challenge you to lay your calendar before God each day. In a spirit of submission, pray through each appointment and activity. Seek His will for the blank spaces in that day's schedule, and fill them with prayer-prompted priorities.

DELEGATING RESPONSIBILITY

Delegation is a critical skill for any leader who wants to minimize the effects of a personal limitation and continue pursuing the mission. Having defined the personal contribution God calls us to make, we must delegate what remains to others. When Joshua divided the remaining territory among the tribes, he essentially delegated to other leaders the responsibility for conquering that land. Up to that point there had been a centralized offensive with Joshua as its leader. Now the battle would move forward under decentralized leadership.

Joshua moved from being a doer to a delegator. That may be a transition we are called to make as well. The more we become involved in equipping (versus ministering as defined earlier), the more indispensable is the art of delegation.

Why is delegation so difficult? The reason is partly practical. It often seems easier to do something myself than to teach another person to do it. But the reason goes deeper—delegation involves trust. Am I willing to trust others with not only the responsibility but also the authority to carry out critical dimensions of the mission?

The development of trust requires a mutual contribution. The one who receives responsibility must be trustworthy. Faithfully discharging smaller responsibilities will lead to being entrusted with more (Luke 16:10). The one who delegates authority must be trusting. And trust always involves risk, so the delegator must be willing to take a reasonable risk in order to provide an opportunity for someone else to succeed. As the one given responsibility achieves the desired result, a new level of trust is created, paving the way for even greater successes.

Three dimensions of delegation increase the likelihood of success.

DIMENSION ONE: DELEGATE RESULTS, NOT TASKS

God instructed Joshua to divide up the Promised Land among the tribes of Israel, giving the leaders of each tribe the responsibility to conquer that portion of property. Joshua did not prescribe how the tribes were to conquer their territory, only what territory to conquer.

If we delegate tasks, we simply tell people what do. That keeps them dependent upon us. They go off to do their task, then return to us to report that the task is completed and receive another. If a problem arises, they return to us to solve it. While it may feed the ego to be the "answer person," this is the least effective form of delegation.

On the other hand, if we delegate the results, we are specifying the goal to be accomplished, leaving it to the individual to determine how it should be done. As leaders, we provide a vision of what is to be accomplished. We also provide broad parameters of authority within which the mission must be fulfilled. Others then provide the strategies for accomplishing the vision within those broad-stroke boundaries. While some of their strategies may fail, this form of delegation empowers people to be successful independently. It develops them as leaders, not just doers.

When delegation does not produce the desired result, an initial response may be to fault the other person. We should resist that tendency and instead look at the content of our communication. If people don't understand what the desired results are and why they are important, they're likely to pursue their own goals for their own reasons. If I can't communicate the result I do want, I'll get the result I don't want.

DIMENSION TWO: CREATE SYSTEMS FOR SUCCESS

Not People Dependent

Every organization has systems that sustain its life and vitality. The Church Universal, for instance, is called the body of Christ and is compared to a human body. A body has certain systems—such as circulatory, nervous, and reproductive—to sustain itself. In the same way, a local church must have certain systems to ensure good health.

Our church's mission is to reach out and raise up. There are systems in place to support that mission—systems for discipleship, equipping, assimilation, and other functions. The key to creating successful systems is to make them process dependent rather than people dependent.

For instance, consider your system for assimilation, moving people being from first-time visitors to fully contributing members of your church. If your system depends on the heroic effort of a few uniquely gifted individuals, it will fall apart when those people are no longer involved. However, if your assimilation system has several clearly defined steps that involve a number of people at a level appropriate to their gifts, then assimilation will continue after a change in personnel, even after a change in leaders.

Our church had a person who was gifted in recruiting teams of people to serve in short-term missions endeavors. However, he did much of it personally and became the go-to person for any problem or question. The more successful he was in recruiting teams, the less effectively the system worked. It was person dependent. Once the steps of preparing for a missions trip were clearly identified and the desired results specified, many people could take a slice of the responsibility. The system became process dependent, which allowed for the delegation of responsibility to others.

DIMENSION THREE: DELEGATE AS MUCH AS POSSIBLE

When Joshua finished delegating, all the territory had been assigned to others. He did not leave any territory for himself to conquer. He gave away all of the authority and responsibility along with the territory. Many leaders set out to delegate results but wind up with a long list of personal responsibilities. A leader must let people be responsible for their own successes and failures. When people come to you for a solution, don't provide the answer. Ask them to diagnose the situation and arrive at their own solution. Equip them to solve their own problems. Once you have delegated everything, you will be free to do what is most important for a leader to do—identify new opportunities for mission fulfillment.

Personal insecurity causes us to cling unnecessarily to the achievement of results that can be obtained by others. To "give it all away" make us feel vulnerable and dispensable. Yet if we devote that newly freed time and energy to achieving the next thing God calls us to do, we make a greater contribution to the mission.

DEVELOPING RESOURCES

Leaders who have defined their unique contribution and delegated the authority and responsibility for results are free to spend their time and energy developing the resources that are needed to fulfill the mission. The greatest of those resources is people. Some of those people are already serving faithfully alongside you. They need your blessing. Others will emerge under your leadership. They need encouragement.

BLESS EXISTING LEADERS

When Joshua was a much younger man, he was one of twelve commissioned by Moses to scout the Promised Land (Num. 13–14). Of the twelve, he was one of only two who brought back a positive report. Who was the other? A man named Caleb. It was Caleb who silenced the grumbling after everyone was disheartened by the negative report from the other ten spies. It was Caleb who expressed certainty that the Israelites could indeed take possession of the Promised Land (Num. 13:31). Caleb and Joshua were partners in giving a faith-filled report of the possibilities that lay before Israel.

Now, Joshua was very old and had to adopt a new approach to conquering the remaining territory of Canaan. Who would step forward to inspire others and provide an example of leadership? His old partner, Caleb. Forty-five years had passed, but Caleb was as anxious as ever to join Joshua in the quest to conquer the land:

> I am still as strong today as the day Moses sent me out; I'm just as vigorous to go out to battle now as I was then. Now give me this hill country that the LORD promised me that day. You yourself heard then that the Anakites were there and their cities were large and fortified, but, the LORD helping me, I will drive them out just as he said (Josh. 14:11–12).

Caleb was willing to take God at His promise and drive out whoever stood in his way. What an inspiration to the leaders of other tribes and clans!

What was Joshua's response to Caleb's request? Joshua blessed Caleb and gave him his inheritance. Joshua rightly recognized the presence of a proven leader. Caleb needed no training, only the freedom to do what God had called him to do.

Part of my role as a leader is to recognize and bless proven leaders in the expansion of their mission. I have compiled a list of the leaders in our church who are making the greatest contribution to our mission. In addition to praying for them regularly, I review the list on a quarterly basis, asking how I might "bless" them in the months ahead. I may write a simple note of encouragement to one of them. To another, I might make recognition of a success in his or her area of ministry. It could be that I would seek input from one or two of them about a new ministry idea, then listen carefully and appreciatively to their response. I try to discern what would be meaningful to each of them and bless them by providing it if I can.

In our eagerness to identify emerging leaders we must not neglect existing leaders who have been faithful in the past and may well be champing at the bit for a new challenge. This does not mean that we burden already busy people with meaningless activity. It means that we offer them new areas of ministry or new levels of opportunity within their current place of service. Offering leaders a new challenge frees them to act upon God's promises in courageous ways.

The partnership of Joshua and Caleb is one of co-leadership. Warren Bennis, one of the foremost thinkers in the study of leadership, has written a book called *Co-Leaders*.[3] In it he examines the achievements of people who partnered together in order to accomplish more than either could have accomplished alone. In most cases, one partner was more visible, but both were equally valuable.

I enjoy the benefits of such a partnership. Jerry DeRuiter, former mayor of our city and leader of a large social service agency, had served our church effectively in many volunteer capacities. I had been blessed by his leadership on our board and had worked closely with him in increasing the board's efficiency. During his tenure as vice-chairman, we re-engineered our organization to pursue our mission more effectively. That resulted in the creation of a position titled director of church operations. The person who would fill that role would work closely with the senior pastor. As we developed the position, Jerry felt a call upon his heart to apply for it. He stepped away from his involvement in creating the job and obeyed God by applying for it. His love for our church and set of skills made him perfectly suited for the job, and he was hired. Now we serve together as co-leaders in many of the most crucial areas of our church's life. The partnership existed already, but God moved it to a new level.

Build up Emerging Leaders

When he assigned the unconquered territories to the various tribes and clans, Joshua was empowering their leaders to step up to a new responsibility. In so doing he took leaders who had been faithful in a lesser responsibility—leading a tribe or clan—and gave them the opportunity to be faithful in something greater—conquering territory for the tribe or clan.

The Bible is realistic in portraying the various levels of success achieved by these emerging leaders. The leaders of the tribe of Judah could not dislodge the Jebusites from Jerusalem (Josh. 15:63). The leaders of the tribe of Ephraim were not able to eradicate the Canaanites from Gezer but settled for making them do forced labor (Josh. 16:10). These partial victories remind us that equipping leaders for new levels of responsibility is not a no-risk proposition.

Leaders are learners, and learning involves faith. Exercising faith involves risk, and risk implies the possibility of failure. When emerging leaders feel threatened by the possibility of retribution for failure, they become timid. They live within the comfort of the proven possible. They find ways not to perform so that they will not fail. But if they do not fail, they cannot learn. Emerging leaders need encouragement to continue on the right paths and coaching to identify and avoid wrong paths.

Dick Zalack, who has studied the role of the coach extensively, has identified four steps in successful coaching:

1. Communicate the expected result to team members.

2. Show them the result by achieving it yourself.

3. Watch them attempt to achieve the result.

4. Praise their success or redirect them back through the process.

All successful coaches, no matter what their field, follow these four action steps.[4]

Personally, I have found the most difficult part of coaching to be asking questions rather than providing answers. Answering questions may produce a solution, but asking questions produces leaders who create solutions on their own. Being the answer man may be good for my ego, but it's lousy for equipping. When someone encounters a problem and comes to me for the answer, I'm learning to ask questions rather than dispense advice. What are the options? What would be the results, intended or otherwise, from pursuing each option? Which option do you think is best? What could you do to make it better? Guiding leaders through the process of arriving at their own answers is the best long-term strategy for leadership development.

Sometimes emerging leaders want greater reward without accepting greater responsibility. Joshua encountered that attitude in the leaders of the people of Joseph (Josh. 17:14–18). They rightly acknowledged that God had blessed them and made them numerous. They requested more territory based on this "blessing." Joshua did assign additional territory to them, but it was occupied by the Canaanites, whom the people of Joseph found intimidating. When assigning the additional territory, Joshua reaffirmed that the people of Joseph were numerous. The blessing they had cited as a reason for seeking greater reward was the same blessing Joshua cited in challenging them to conquer more territory—"You are numerous and very powerful . . . though they are strong, you will drive them out." He wanted them to use their strengths to accomplish something, to further God's mission rather than demand an entitlement.

In both blessing existing leaders and empowering emerging leaders, the character of the subordinate leader is critically important. It's amazing how many spiritual leaders neglect the character issue when enamored with a young leader's experience or skills. It is far easier to teach skill to a person of character than it is to change the character of someone who is highly skilled. Character first. Commitment second. Competence third.

Reaching Beyond the Limit

In spite of Joshua's personal limitation, the vast remaining mission was accomplished:

> So the LORD gave Israel all the land he had sworn to give their forefathers, and they took possession of it and settled there. The LORD gave them rest on every side, just as he had sworn to their forefathers. Not one of their enemies withstood them; the LORD handed all their enemies over to them. Not one of all the LORD's good promises to the house of Israel failed; every one was fulfilled (Josh. 21:43–45).

Sometimes God moves slowly so that we will recognize our limitations and learn how to transcend them in order to fulfill our God-given mission.

I've seen that both in my life and in the lives of those on our staff team. For instance, Mark Carroll, who leads our youth ministry, has been loving and serving students for a quarter century. When he began in youth ministry, he was a single guy in his early twenties. He spent all his time with the kids—he was both their pastor and big brother!

Then he served a youth ministry of nearly a hundred kids for several years. He was now married and raising a family of his own. He trained a few of the students to provide leadership within the youth group, but Mark was still the primary adult minister to the whole group.

Now Mark leads a youth ministry that includes three other staff members, more than a hundred adult lay ministers, and many student leaders. He still loves kids (though we razz him about being more of a father figure now than a big brother). Serving with him is a management team of highly skilled leaders who handle the logistics of the ministry, freeing him to fulfill his passion to directly impact the lives of students.

Mark freely admits that the transition to each new stage was a struggle. Although a quarter century has passed, he is still doing what he loves. More important, he is fulfilling God's call upon his life. His vision is for the youth department to minister to a thousand students each week, yet that goal is well beyond the boundary of his personal limitations. He has found a way to manage those limitations and still fulfill a vast remaining mission. He inspires me to do the same.

PERSONAL REFLECTION

1. What personal limitations do you have? What might you do to manage or minimize them?

2. Is God prompting or leading you in any way right now? What are you doing in response?

3. What spiritual disciplines are you building into your life to make it more likely that you will sense and obey God's leading?

4. When you look back over your life, do you see a pattern in the way God has led you? Toward what does God seem to consistently lead you?

5. Trusting others can be a huge hurdle for leaders to cross. Do you find it easy or difficult to trust others? What factors (for example, past experiences or personality) may be limiting your ability to trust others?

6. Do you have any insecurities that keep you from blessing and empowering others? What are those insecurities, and in what ways might God work in your life to overcome them?

INVENTORY FOR SPIRITUAL LEADERS

1. Have you every tried to limit the mission God has given you so it would fit within your limitations? If so, how have you done that, and how might you avoid doing it in the future?

2. Complete the exercises included in the "Defining Your Role" section of this chapter. Identify two things that have become more clear to you about yourself and your role as a leader.

3. How do you rate yourself in the area of delegation? In what ways might you strengthen your skills in this area?

4. List some of your existing leaders. Name one way that you can bless each of them.

5. Name some of your emerging leaders. Think of one thing you can do to empower each of them.

—ɯ—

JOSHUA'S JOURNAL

Lord, You are the Creator, with unlimited knowledge, power, and life. I am a creature with very real limitations. While these limitations may seem burdensome to me, may they never limit the mission that You desire to accomplish. Please show me the contribution You want me to make, and then enable me to let go of those things that are beyond my reach. May I trust, bless, and support others who join me in Your great kingdom work. Amen.

CHAPTER SEVEN

THE CRUCIBLE

OF CONFLICT

—〰—

STALL FACTOR: Unresolved conflict.
FORWARD STEP: Engage conflict faithfully.

I have the privilege of serving on a board that involves me in the ministry of many churches beyond the one I serve. As a result, I sometimes receive behind-the-scenes insight into situations faced by other spiritual leaders. Having served on this board off and on for many years, I sense that church conflict is becoming more common. Certainly the presence of multiple generations within many local churches is one factor contributing to this increase. Another is the consumer mind-set with which many people shop for churches and often retain after joining. That what's-in-this-for-me attitude seems to give people the freedom to express what they like and what they don't. The disappearance of

If passion drives you, let reason hold the reins.

—Benjamin Franklin

Peacemakers who sow in peace raise a harvest of righteousness.

—James 3:18

denominational loyalty has created a situation in which people are aware of many different ministry styles and have higher expectations for the scope and quality of services that a local church should provide.

Recently the board on which I serve dealt with a situation where a plateaued local church had called an energetic young pastor. The young man was initially greeted with enthusiasm, but it wasn't long before some of the changes he implemented were resisted by some long-term members. People chose sides, as people will, and those on each side considered their anger with the other to be "righteous indignation." Labels were applied to the viewpoints of others. The situation escalated to the point where some members were perceived as winners and others as losers. In the end, the pastor remained as leader while many long-term members left the church. It could have easily ended the other way around. Sadly, ill-managed conflict once again resulted in division.

There are many surprises in the life of a spiritual leader. One of those surprises is how quickly a group of people can move from celebration to conflict. One day they may communicate affirmation and the next day radiate suspicion. The distance between unity and disunity is incredibly short and all too easily traveled.

Joshua saw that principle powerfully at work shortly after God declared the conquest of the Promised Land to be complete (Josh. 21:43–45). The conquest was made possible, in part, because the Reubenites, the Gadites, and the half tribe of Manasseh, who had been assigned territory on the east side of the Jordan, had fulfilled their promise to assist the other tribes in subduing the nations on the west side (Josh. 22:1–9). Moses had assigned eastern territory to those two and a half tribes on the condition that they agree to do just that (Num. 32:16–33). Moses clearly communicated that condition to Joshua, Eleazar the priest, and the family heads of the Israelite tribes.

Now that the conquest was complete, Joshua publicly declared that the eastern tribes had fulfilled their commitment and sent them home with the plunder they had earned. They departed with the satisfaction of having kept their promise and with the prosperity God bestowed upon their faithful labor. But by the time they reached the Jordan River, conflict erupted.

THE VALUE OF CONFLICT RESOLUTION

While most of us enjoy the celebrations of ministry, few of us enjoy the conflicts. Recognizing and resolving conflict is my Achilles' heel as a leader. Far too often I've either created conflict or avoided it, leaving it unresolved. Conflict resolution is a leadership skill that others have identified as underdeveloped in me, a point at which I need to grow. As I have learned more about conflict resolution and gotten better at doing it, there has been greater unity within our staff members, lay leaders, and congregation.

One of the reasons God sometimes moves slowly is to allow for conflict resolution. This resolution can take a good deal of time, but if conflict is left unresolved, it will consume even more time and energy later on. Resolving conflict is a matter of paying now or paying more later.

There are two extreme views of conflict. One is that all conflict is harmful, even sinful. By this reasoning, conflict is to be avoided at any cost. That thinking causes many people to live in denial, ignoring the reality of conflict. Rather than true peace, it results in a cease-fire or truce. Conflict becomes the "elephant in the room"—everyone knows it is there, but no one will acknowledge it. Left unaddressed, conflict can become chronic, even terminal, for a movement of God.

The other extreme view is that all conflict is helpful. It is to be expected and embraced as a godly means of building up the fellowship God's people. Every confrontation is seen as an opportunity to deepen relationships and develop the ministry. This thinking may cause some people to escalate conflict, needlessly expending time and energy that would be better devoted to higher causes.

I believe the biblical view of conflict lies somewhere between these two extremes. This view is displayed in the Scriptures, one of them being Col. 3:13: "Bear with each other and forgive whatever grievances you may have against one another. Forgive as the Lord forgave you." This verse calls for forbearance so that not every difference of opinion is viewed as a conflict. It also calls for forgiveness in cases where the conflict is serious.

Forbearance is an old word but a good one. It reminds us that every perceived slight or rash word should not become a source of conflict. If every offense, no matter how minor, were viewed as a threat to a relationship, it wouldn't be long before the people in any group would tire of one another. "Bear with one another" is a biblical expression roughly equivalent to the maxim "Don't sweat the small stuff, and most of it is small stuff."

There are times when conflict can be avoided with integrity. A meeting may become emotionally charged or a person may be defensive in a conversation. If a time-out is taken and an opportunity for reflection given, those involved will likely adopt an attitude of forbearance and conclude that their initial reaction was not the best response. Forbearance tempers raw emotion with spiritual wisdom.

Forgiveness is needed when an offense has gone deeper. The expression "forgive and forget" does not serve us well. To simply forget about a conflict is an act of forbearance. What we cannot forget must be forgiven. These are insults that are too painful or damaging to be avoided with integrity. To do so would be to shut down a part of our soul, creating fertile soil for the root of bitterness to take hold. When deeply wounded, we must come to the point of offering forgiveness; we must "forgive as Christ forgave us." Forgiveness does not always lead to reconciliation. To fully recover a relationship depends on mutual participation in the process of conflict resolution. One person can forgive. It takes two to be reconciled.

The conflict that erupted between the tribes of Israel could not be avoided with integrity (Josh. 22:10–34). Although it was based on an misperception, this conflict shows that the tribes of Israel cared deeply about their unity and did not want a geographical boundary—the Jordan River—to become a relational or spiritual barrier between them. Conflicts probably occur more frequently where people care more deeply. As Larry McSwain and William C. Treadwell Jr. observe:

> Conflict occurs most often in congregations in which there is a deep commitment to the church. The more deeply ingrained the sense of ownership about what is happening, the more possible is conflict. Apathy is a sure guarantee of a conflict-free setting. Persons who do not care about their faith are unlikely to exhibit enough energy to act upon it. Corpses do not fight![1]

The successful resolution of Israel's conflict would produce greater unity. The conflict had the potential, if not resolved successfully, to escalate into civil war, perhaps weakening Israel to the point that it could not maintain occupation of the Promised Land.

SOURCES OF CONFLICT

Conflict can arise from many different sources. Just as a medical doctor must make a diagnosis before writing a prescription, so the source of a conflict must be diagnosed before a resolution can be determined. A brief survey of conflicts described in the New Testament reveals at least four sources.

SOURCE ONE: PERSONAL ISSUES

Conflict may begin within an individual who then projects his or her internal conflict upon an external situation. James poses this question: "What causes fights and quarrels among you?" He then answers his own question, "Don't they come from your desires that battle within you? You want something but you don't get it. You kill and covet, but you can not have what you want. You quarrel and fight." (James 4:1–2). Troubled people cause trouble. A troublemaker is the opposite of a peacemaker.

I must admit that I occasionally allow turmoil within me to spill into the situation around me. When that happens, someone who loves me is always gracious enough to pull me aside and ask what's really bothering me. Usually, I'm initially defensive and continue to project my feelings onto the situation. But loving persistence leads me to admit that my feelings are completely unrelated to the "conflict." I've pulled others aside to ask that same question, so I know this happens even among the most mature Christians.

But some people are chronically troubled. They may have unresolved bitterness, untreated mental illness, or perhaps have given Satan a foothold in their lives through continual anger. There is a long list of possible reasons. These high-maintenance people create conflict wherever they go. They, too, must be brought to understand that the source of conflict is within them.

Willingness to look within is a mark of humility and paves the road to freedom. If a troubled person is unable or unwilling to examine internal conflicts, we as spiritual leaders must minimize the impact they have on others and marginalize their influence on the group. A troubled person should not be placed in a leadership role.

SOURCE TWO: PRIORITY DIFFERENCES

Conflict can occur when people have different priorities. This is not an issue of sin or selfishness, but a genuine difference of opinion about where resources should be invested. This was the situation in Acts 6:1–7. The church was growing rapidly and had outgrown the apostles' ability to meet the needs of all believers. As a result, certain widows were being neglected in the daily distribution of food. The apostles decided that their first priorities should be prayer and the ministry of the Word of God. Yet they affirmed the validity of supporting widows and proposed that seven men "full of the Holy Spirit and wisdom" be chosen to handle the responsibility to distribute food.

This proposal was well-received by the whole group. Seven men were chosen, which resulted in an increase in the number of leaders. It also permitted the unhindered spread of the gospel, which resulted in an increase in the number of disciples in Jerusalem. This conflict was resolved by finding a way for the right people to address the priorities that would sustain this fresh movement of God.

Most growing movements experience a clash of priorities because they have limited resources of time, money, and energy. This type of conflict is predictable and can be very productive by stimulating involvement in the mission by others. Leaders are wise to avoid seeing priority conflicts as issues of right and wrong or spiritualizing the conflict. They do well to see such disputes as questions of who, what, and when and seek answers that promote all of the God-honoring priorities.

As I write these words we're working through the challenge of prioritizing our ministry opportunities. Occasions for ministry are abounding at a time when financial resources are somewhat limited. It would be easy to engage in turf wars between ministry departments. And it's tempting simply to distribute resources evenly so that everybody gets a little but nobody gets enough. That would avoid some tension, but we're more interested in completing our mission. So we're setting priorities, identifying the ministries that are mission-critical for our church, and providing their necessary resources first. Other initiatives will be funded as our financial situation allows. While we risk some conflict, we know that the resolution of that conflict will produce a more focused and fruitful ministry.

SOURCE THREE: PERSPECTIVE VARIANCES

Different people can look at the same person or situation and arrive at completely different conclusions. Such was the case with Barnabas and Paul, who couldn't agree on whether Mark should accompany them on another missionary journey (Acts 15:36–41). Mark had previously deserted them, not following through on his assignment. Barnabas, always the encourager, wanted to give Mark a second chance. Paul, who could never understand anything less that full devotion, thought it unwise to trust Mark a second time. The disagreement between Barnabas and Paul became so sharp that they eventually decided to go their separate ways.

Happily, that resulted in two missionary journeys instead of one. Barnabas took Mark and sailed for Cyprus. Paul was joined by Silas and traveled through Syria and Cilicia strengthening the churches. While Paul and Barnabas did not share the same perspective, neither did they disparage one another. In fact, near the end of his life Paul had seen such a change in Mark and come to appreciate him so much that he asked for Mark to attend him during his final days (2 Tim. 4:11). Was Barnabas right and Paul wrong? That's not the issue, and it seldom is in resolving conflicts of perspective. Resolution depends on maintaining respect for those who hold a different view while continuing to work—perhaps separately—for the advance of the gospel. Sometimes it's best to "agree to disagree," then shift attention from the dissension to the mission.

SOURCE FOUR: PRINCIPLE CENTERED

Principle-centered conflicts can occur when one person has sinned against another. This is the source of conflict Jesus had in mind in Matt. 18:15–17. Jesus described the process for resolving these conflicts, instructing us first to approach the offending party and point out the fault. If that person responds, the conflict is solved. If the person will not listen, however, we are to enlist the aid of another person or two and try again to resolve the situation. If the person still refuses to respond, then the matter is to be brought before the church for action.

If someone comes to me to discuss a situation where another person has sinned against him, at the earliest possible moment in the conversation I ask whether he has confronted that person already. If the answer is no, I make it clear that confronting that person personally is his next step. I then offer to pray for the situation, asking God to give a clear voice and a listening ear. If the situation is really based on a misunderstanding, I ask God to bring that to light so that both parties can see it. I also pray that the offending person will have a responsive heart and, if the situation calls for it, a repentant spirit. Only after the initial step of personal confrontation has been taken does our church's conflict resolution team become involved in seeking resolution.

Principle-centered conflict may involve a group of people as opposed to two individuals. When a principle is at stake, it must be publicly discussed and resolved. Such was the case in Acts 15 when the Jerusalem Council met to discuss the role of Jewish law in the lives of Christians. Some Jewish Christians argued that gentile Christians should observe the law as a sign of their true acceptance of Christ—circumcision, as taught by Moses, was a requirement for salvation. Others, notably the Apostle Paul, disagreed. They believed that in Christ we are free from the requirements of the law. Conflict arising from differing value systems is the deepest and most difficult kind. People will kill and be killed for principles they see as non-negotiable.

At the Jerusalem Council, background information was openly presented. Then the apostles and elders met to consider the issue. Finally, the Apostle Peter, undoubtedly the one who spoke with greatest authority to Jewish Christians, announced the Council's decision—a compromise which allowed Gentiles to come freely to Christ but asked that they defer to Jewish sensibilities on certain matters. The Council's open approach to resolving this dispute avoided schism while preserving the central value of Christianity—salvation through faith in Christ alone.

RESOLVING CONFLICT

The conflict that unfolds in Joshua, chapter 22, sprang from two sources—perspective and principle. It is not unusual to have two or more sources of conflict overlapping in one event.

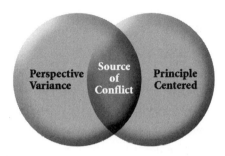

Conflict arose when the eastern tribes built an imposing altar near the Jordan river (22:10). Ever since the encampment at Sinai, the Israelites had had a centralized place of worship, the Tabernacle. The construction of alternate places of worship was expressly forbidden by God. The western tribes viewed this act of devotion by their kinsmen as a violation of God's command. What was intended as a declaration of unity was misinterpreted as act of rebellion.

The process by which this conflict was resolved yields helpful guidelines for resolving most conflicts that involve a group of people.

STEP ONE: SELECT A TEAM (JOSH. 22:13–14)

First, a representative group from the western tribes was selected to initiate communication with the eastern tribes. When a conflict involves a large group of people (in this case, an entire nation) it's usually best to refer it to an appropriate team of people. The role of that team must be carefully defined. Will it be to facilitate discussion only, to make a recommendation, or to decide on a resolution? In Israel's case, the team was commissioned to seek an interview and report back on the reason behind the eastern tribes' construction of the altar.

The team was led by a spiritual leader—Phineas the son of Eleazar the priest. Its membership included ten chief men, one from each of the nine and a half western tribes, so it was a representative group. If representatives are chosen, they must represent the whole group, not just their own "tribe." And they must be qualified to contribute to the process, not chosen merely to get a representative from each "tribe."

Referring conflict to a team may prolong the process of resolution, but it may also diffuse the tension. When the western tribes heard about the altar, they mobilized for war against the eastern tribes. Their first impulse was to do battle. The time it took for the team to do its investigative work provided a cooling-off period when calmer minds could prevail. Using the team method can move a conflict from an emotion-charged setting to a more rational footing, which is especially helpful during the information gathering phase.

Our church has a conflict resolution team that follows a process approved by our governing board. The team's members have been equipped to be peacemakers. They understand both the biblical basis and practical framework for conflict resolution. We have found that the best team members do not take conflict personally—they are not paralyzed by the thought of being personally disliked or having their ideas rejected. Peacemakers must be patient with a process that can be highly ambiguous and frustrating. They must also be neutral, entering the situation without a personal agenda, in order to have credibility with all sides involved.

STEP TWO: COMMUNICATE CONCERNS (JOSH. 22:15–18)

The team appointed by the western tribes entered an emotionally charged situation where they communicated their concern by asking questions. Those questions belied their assumptions, which was not an ideal tactic. Their questions began in an accusatory manner, but ended by showing at least some willingness to listen.

- "How could you break faith with the God of Israel like this?"

- "How could you turn away from the LORD and build yourselves an altar in rebellion against him now?"

- "Was not the sin of Peor enough for us?"

- "And are you now turning away from the LORD?"

During this information gathering phase of their conflict resolution, the team attempted both to clarify their own position and to understand the perspective of the eastern tribes. The first two questions clarified their position. The third question cited a historical precedent for their concern, referring to a time when some Israelites became involved in an inappropriate form of worship—worship to the detriment of the entire nation. The last question inquired into the motivation behind the eastern tribes' action.

This interview is the first engagement between the two conflicting groups. McSwain and Treadwell describe some unhealthy strategies for dealing with confrontation.

Fright. Some people are so afraid of conflict that they refuse to acknowledge its presence. The underlying assumption is that the conflict will go away if ignored.

Flight. Flight is withdrawal from the arena of conflict. Some examples of that in church conflicts are the withdrawal of membership, the withholding of financial support, or nonparticipation in church activities.

Fight. Fighting may include a variety of actions. Repression is a form of fighting where the majority constantly overrules the powerless minority. Subversion is a type of fighting in which the minority tries to undermine the majority or leadership by exaggerating issues or assassinating character.[2]

Because the eastern and western tribes were on the brink of battle, the questioning phase was crucial for avoiding unhealthy fighting by either side. By asking questions, the western tribes initiated a healthy problem resolution strategy that would provide the freedom to arrive at a solution.

Healthy conflict resolution begins with communication. Each side must make a clear statement of the need or goal behind its concern. The more ways in which that communication is given, the more likely it is to be understood.

STEP THREE: CONCEPTUALIZE POSSIBLE OPTIONS (JOSH. 22:18–20)

The western group clearly communicated the fact that they saw the construction of this altar as a matter that would affect the entire nation of Israel (22:18). They cited the sin of Achan to illustrate the point (22:20). They reminded their brethren of the fact that God looked upon them as one nation, not as separate entities divided by a river. If judgement was to come, it would come upon all. By defining the danger as all-inclusive—it would affect the eastern and the western tribes—they avoided casting the debate in us-versus-them terms.

Then they offered a solution to the eastern group that demonstrated a willingness to sacrifice: "If the land you possess is defiled . . . share the land with us" (22:19). Although the land west of the Jordan had been apportioned to the nine-and-a-half tribes, they were more than willing to share it with the other two-and-a-half tribes in order to prevent any inappropriate worship and the judgement it would surely bring. The western tribes probably felt that they were offering a superior property to the eastern tribes because God had clearly identified the Promised Land as west of the Jordan. Their offer reflected the gracious spirit that is necessary in diffusing any conflict.

The process had begun with the western tribes ready to go to war. Their make-them-pay attitude gave way to a let-us-help spirit as they offered to move over and make room in the Promised Land. The movement from an us-versus-them to a we're-in-this-together mentality always creates a climate conducive to conflict resolution.

STEP FOUR: LISTEN TO THE RESPONSE OF THOSE CONFRONTED (JOSH. 22:21–29)

After offering a solution, the western tribes allowed the others to respond. They began by reaffirming their commitment to the shared value system of the Israelite tribes. They did that in three ways. First, they acknowledged the rightful place of their mighty God and gave Him praise. Next, they affirmed that God understood their true motivation for building the altar—it was not an act of rebellion or disobedience

(22:22). Third, they agreed that if their motive had been a rebellious one, action that the western tribes were planning to take would have been warranted. That statement demonstrated their willingness to be accountable for their actions (22:23). These affirmations must have begun to put the western tribes at ease. They also indicated that the group's concerns had been clearly heard.

Having established that common ground, the eastern tribes provided the explanation for their action.

First, their motive was to prevent future generations from viewing the Jordan river as a spiritual barrier (22:24–25). The altar was intended as a symbol of solidarity with the main body of Israelites.

Second, the altar was not a place for making sacrifices but was a reminder that the eastern tribes worshiped the same God and should always have access to the sacrificial altar located on the western side of the river (22:26–28).

Third, rather than a symbol of rebellion, the altar was intended to be a permanent reminder that there was only one acceptable place to make burnt offerings and that all the people of Israel should have access to it (22:29).

All of these explanations support the statement by the eastern tribes that their true motive was to honor God.

From our vantage point, it's obvious that mistaken assumptions contributed to the development of this conflict. The western tribes assumed that the altar had been constructed for burnt offerings—it hadn't. The eastern tribes assumed that future generations of western Israelites would use the geographical boundary of the Jordan against them—there is no objective reason to believe that they would have. If either side had communicated clearly before the altar was constructed, there would have been no conflict.

As they talked and listened to one another, both groups communicated in emotion and action. They went beyond simply reporting the facts—which is vitally important—to communicate their feelings. Both the content (what happened) and the context (how we feel about it) must be communicated if reconciliation is to take place.

STEP FIVE: DETERMINE IF THE RESPONSES ARE CREDIBLE (JOSH. 22:30–33)

The explanation offered by the eastern tribes was accepted. The response of Phinehas and the other leaders shows that they were pleased by what they heard (22:30). They recognized the hand of God in the conflict resolution process and were convinced that the conclusion honored Him (22:31).

The western delegation then completed their assignment. Since they had been commissioned to communicate concerns and then report back, they returned home to make their accounting. Upon hearing the report, the whole assembly was pleased and used the occasion to give glory to God (22:32–33).

STEP SIX: CLOSURE (JOSH. 22:34)

The eastern tribes brought closure to this conflict through a symbolic act. They named the altar "A Witness between Us That the LORD is God." It's a long name, but it addressed all the concerns of both parties to the conflict. For the eastern tribes, it provided a reminder that all Israelites must have access to the altar of sacrifice in Canaan. For the western tribe, it affirmed that the altar was intended to be a symbol, not a place of worship. For all the tribes, it publicly declared that "the LORD is God," putting them on record against the pagan practice of worshiping many gods in many places.

We rarely terminate our conflicts today by erecting or naming altars. But there are other spiritually significant symbolic acts that can seal the resolution of a dispute. What if all sides observed communion together? Or participated in a foot-washing service or time of prayer around the altar? Wouldn't it be refreshing if all parities made a common statement affirming their shared values and conclusions? In these symbolic ways, or others, we add a vertical dimension to conflict resolution.

Celebrating the fact that the conflict is ended may also be helpful.

That celebration might take the form of a shared meal, a praise service, or the offering of affirmation to those who took part in the resolution. Celebration serves not only as a source of encouragement for those involved but also as a witness to others who may have observed the dispute.

These steps to conflict resolution works best when taken in order. It's tempting to jump ahead, discussing options before the concerns are clearly identified, or declaring closure before true resolution has been reached. Slow-motion times allow us to follow the process carefully, all the way to completion.

The leaders of our church have developed a conflict resolution flow chart, which identifies the questions to ask and steps to take in resolving a conflict. That's helpful, because once we're in the heat of a disagreement, we have a clear roadmap that directs us toward the steps to resolution.

PERSONAL REFLECTION

1. What is your view of conflict?

   ⟵——————————————————⟶

   Harmful   Helpful

   Why do you view conflict as you do?

2. Do you know anyone who requires a high level of forbearance? How do you deal with that person?

3. Is there someone you need to forgive?

4. Are you now involved in any conflict in your personal life? What do you see are the sources of that conflict?

   _____ Personal Issues
   _____ Priority Differences
   _____ Perspective Variances
   _____ Principles

5. What emotions do you tend to experience during conflict? How do those emotions affect your involvement in conflict resolution?

INVENTORY FOR SPIRITUAL LEADERS

1. In the early stages of a conflict, people tend to choose sides. What steps might a leader take to prevent division when conflict begins?

2. If it can be done with integrity, it is sometimes best for a leader to avoid a conflict. What is the difference between avoiding conflict with integrity and avoiding it because it is difficult or undesirable?

3. Review the four sources of conflict. Can you identify conflicts you've experienced as a leader that arose from each source?

    Personal Issues:

    Priority Differences:

    Perspective Variances:

    Principle Centered:

4. If you were to appoint a conflict resolution team, whom would you include? What qualities do these people possess that makes you think of them as potential peacemakers?

5. Do you have a conflict resolution flow chart or pathway for resolving conflicts? What action steps would you recommend to someone who was facing a conflict?

JOSHUA'S JOURNAL

Lord, life is full of conflict. Help me to know which ones to avoid as an act of forbearance and which conflicts I must help resolve. Give me the discernment to know the source of each conflict, and prevent my judgment from being clouded by unmanaged emotions or false assumptions. In every situation, may I be part of the solution and not part of the problem because of my actions and attitudes. May I be a peacemaker. Amen.

CHAPTER EIGHT

A LEADER'S LEGACY

—·w·—

> **STALL FACTOR:** Failure to plan for transition.
> **FORWARD STEP:** Lead well until you leave well.

I magine giving your farewell speech. Not just a farewell speech at the conclusion of your career. A farewell speech that publicly concludes your life. The last two chapters of Joshua record such a speech. Joshua's words cause me to reflect on what my words will be when the time comes for my farewell. That little exercise is actually a valuable habit for leaders and one espoused by Stephen Covey in his book *Seven Habits of Highly Effective People*. That habit? "Begin with the end in mind."[1]

I pen these words on the eve of the 2002 Leadership Summit. Our church is a simulcast site for this highly acclaimed event sponsored by Willow Creek Community Church. I'll

Things which matter most must never be at the mercy of things which matter least.

—Johann Wolfgang von Goethe

Now there is in store for me a crown of right-eousness, which the Lord, the righteous Judge, will award to me on that day—and not only to me, but also to all who have longed for his appearing.

—2 Timothy 4:8

never forget the final session of last year's summit. The topic was "Ending Well." During that session, Bill Hybels passed along the words of wisdom that were given to him as he left his first ministry assignment—"You'll be remembered by how you leave."

I'm a student of how people leave. I learn from their examples. Whether they are church members leaving their congregation (sometimes leaving our church, sometimes leaving another to come here), or leaders leaving their ministry assignments, I've taken note of a long line of leavers, and determined what I'd like to do—and not do—when the time comes for me to move on. I've observed some who have made their exit in a classy manner, others in a way that was really petty. As I've listened to their words, I've thought about what I'd like to say—and leave unsaid.

Final words make a lasting impression. I heard of one church where the pastor used his final sermon to preach on the evils of playing cards. It might have been a hot button for him, but that hardly ended his ministry with a life changing message. We don't want to waste final words by majoring on the minors.

Nor should we use final words to settle a score. Many embittered leaders have used their farewell speech as an occasion to blast their enemies, real or imagined. That venting may provide a momentary sense of victory, but it seldom benefits leaders or endears them to the audience. Farewell speeches are best used to lay a foundation for the future, not recount the frustrations of the past.

The Bible records several farewell speeches. Many passages in both the Old and New Testaments are given to such orations. The fact that they are recorded in Scripture indicates their importance. At the ripe old age of 110, Joshua delivered his final address to the leaders of Israel. The centerpiece of the speech is often quoted—"Choose for yourselves this day whom you will serve. . . . but as for me and my household, we will serve the LORD." (Josh. 24:15). There's a lot to learn from the rest of the speech too.

The speech provides an outline that may help us do some advance work on our own farewell presentations, even though they may not be delivered for years to come. Yet I know that if my farewell speech is a work in progress, I'll be more likely to focus attention on the legacy I want to leave. That future focus will help me make decisions about how I want to live today.

Maybe that's another reason God sometimes chooses to move slowly. Rarely do urgent items form the core of one's legacy. Only when we take time for reflection, seeking a release from daily routines, do the items of highest importance come into view. That's another reason I keep a journal during my daily quiet time with God. Journal writing is a spiritual discipline that helps me transcend the everyday and contemplate things of eternal significance.

THE DATE OF DELIVERY

Most of us do not know when we'll give our farewell speech. Maybe we'll never have the chance to deliver it. Perhaps someone will discover our rough drafts and refine them for those we love. For Joshua, the delivery date came at an enviable time, both when his personal limitations had finally caught up with him and when the final chapter of his mission had been written.

Joshua completed the task God had given to him. As the book of Joshua opens, Moses had recently died, and God gave Joshua this commission—"Be strong and courageous, because you will lead these people to inherit the land I swore to their forefathers to give them." (Josh. 1:6). As the record of Joshua's life closes, we're told that his task is completed—"A long time had passed and the LORD had given Israel rest from all their enemies around them" (Josh. 23:1). There was still work to be done, but Joshua's part was over.

One of my favorite verses is found in the High Priestly prayer of Jesus, recorded in John, chapter 17. Verse 4 of that chapter states "I have brought you glory on earth by completing the work you gave me to do." Jesus, too, had accomplished His God-given mission. True, He had gathered only a handful of immature disciples while the entire world was yet to be reached, but Jesus had the satisfaction of knowing that His mission was accomplished. He would make the transition to a ministry of intercession for others, those who would take up the mission from that point forward.

Someday, I want to be able to say that I have accomplished the mission God gave me to do. I hope to look to heaven one day and pray to my Heavenly Father, "I have brought you glory on earth by completing the work you gave me to do." I make no comparison between the perfect Son of God and this far-from-perfect servant. I simply recognize that God has given me work to do, and I hope to recognize also when that work is completed. Then I will aim to begin a ministry of intercession for those who are empowered by God's Spirit to lead the mission from that point forward.

I went to lunch recently with some other pastors. One of them spoke of his sincere struggle to discern whether his present ministry assignment had been completed and the time was right to say farewell. He was considering his own season in life, the present complexity of his church's ministry, and the opportunities and obstacles that lay just ahead. He commented on the many times of prayer he had spent in seeking the will of God. Just then, another in the group piped in about a nearby pastor who had resigned abruptly out of frustration with his congregation. He gave no advance notice to the board or the leaders in his denomination. He announced his resignation on a Sunday morning, and it was effective immediately. I found myself wanting to handle my farewell like the first pastor, not the second. I want my departure to be prompted by prayerful reflection, not overwhelming frustration.

Joshua arrived at this "mission accomplished" point just as his personal limitations asserted their grasp upon his life. He was "by then old and well advanced in years" (Josh. 23:1) and said so to his leadership team (Josh. 23:2). Joshua's energy for leadership had been spent. He understood that his capacities were diminishing.

I pray for that same discernment. I not only pray for it, but I've asked a group of trusted colleagues to help me acquire it. I don't want to be the last one to know that I'm no longer capable of providing the leadership that is needed. These friends have promised that if I don't perceive that moment when it comes, they will lovingly tell me "that I no longer have what it takes to lead at the required level." It may be uncomfortable to hear that message, but it would be preferable by far to the slow torture of becoming increasingly impotent as a leader.

It may be wise for leaders to design a system for soliciting feedback that will transmit signals when others become concerned about their competence. I meet one-to-one each year with the members of our board to receive input on my life and ministry. I try to discern from their comments whether they still believe I'm putting forth the energy needed to lead effectively. I also seek 360-degree feedback, which includes the insight of not only the board that supervises me but also the peers I serve with and people who report to me. This well-rounded input, if received with a humble and teachable spirit, is invaluable for identifying areas of leadership that need attention.

We probably all know leaders who've stayed too long. Some even feel entitled to years of mediocre ministry as a reward for earlier years of productivity. They coast along, reciting their accolades from years gone by. They remain in the position but no longer have passion or fulfill the function. The respect they earned in earlier years is forfeited by their lack of discernment about their diminished capacities.

Joshua's limitations were acknowledged and his assignment completed. It was the right time to say good-bye. Joshua was about to die, and every promise that God made to him on behalf of the people of Israel has been fulfilled. What a way to go.

FACETS OF THE FAREWELL

Joshua's good-bye is a classic. Any leader who wants to begin crafting a farewell address, a statement of the legacy he or she wishes to leave, would do well to use it as a model. Joshua's speech offers seven points that are important to include in any farewell. It prompts me to ask seven questions about the end of my own ministry.

BLESSINGS

What will I count as blessings at the end of my career? Joshua recalled all the benefits the Israelites had received as a result of the Lord's faithfulness (Josh. 23:3). By doing so, he pointed out what they themselves had witnessed and gave glory to God for these good things. Looking back with gratitude would enable Israel to look ahead in faith. Past blessings generate confidence in future endeavors.

Some leaders encounter *blessing blockers*. One blessing blocker is burnout. Many leaders expend their personal well-being in the pursuit of ministry goals that go far beyond their assigned mission. They attempt to do their part, everybody else's part, and God's part too! Burned-out leaders forget how to count blessings—all they can see are the burdens. Grumbling replaces gratitude.

Disappointment is another blessing blocker. By that I mean deep disappointment over serious issues and not the minor let downs that everyone experiences. Someone you trusted or who seemed to have great potential has let you down. Maybe a prayer has gone unanswered or a dream unfulfilled. When those things happen near the end of one's ministry, it's particularly disheartening. But our disappointment with one person who has let us down must not be allowed to block our view of those who have lifted us up. Our dreams that are yet unrealized must not be allowed to undermine our praise for the incredible things that God has already done.

At a recent conference I had two conversations with lay leaders who had left churches in order to serve God in new places. In the first, the lay person spoke highly of those with whom had served at his previous church. He detailed some of the accomplishments they had achieved together. I left the conversation admiring both his positive view of the past and his passion for the future. The second conversation was tinged with bitterness. The lay leader's condescending attitude left me with the impression that he considered the previous church to be beneath him. I left that conversation grateful that he was not part of our church—I was sure that sooner or later we would fail to measure up to his expectations. When someone blesses his past, I admire him. When someone bashes his past, I find myself wanting to avoid serving with him.

I don't advocate viewing life through rose-colored glasses. Anyone involved in the hard work of spiritual leadership knows that there are downsides as well as upsides. In spite of that, intentionally counting our blessings acknowledges God's greatness and affirms His people.

UNFINISHED WORK

Joshua's speech prompts a second question for the close of a ministry. What work is yet to be done? A common trait among leaders is that they are able to see what is yet to be done. The leadership gift includes the ability to recognize goals that are still to be reached and problems yet to be solved. That contributes to the loneliness of leadership; the leader sees what others don't. Joshua used part of his farewell address to remind the Israelites of the land yet to be taken and the enemies yet to be conquered. He also reminded them that God's power would drive these enemies out; God's promises would be fulfilled (Josh. 23:4–5).

Outgoing leaders offer a gift to their successors when they identify the challenges that remain. Retiring leaders demonstrate humility when they avoid giving the impression that everything worth doing has already been done. That gives emerging leaders the opportunity to make a contribution. The next generation can then do more than maintain the glory of the good old days. They can build on the foundation that has been laid.

When stepping out of leadership, it's important to consider both the blessings of the past and the challenges of the future. If a leader considers only the blessings, it's easy for complacency to take root. If a leader considers only the challenges, there is no celebration of past accomplishments and therefore no momentum generated for new ones.

Dick Zalack, personal and professional effectiveness coach, calls this GAP management.[2] He has observed that leaders tend to focus on how far they have yet to go and ignore how far they have come. Leaders are keenly aware of the "gap" between the current reality and the preferred future. Zalack likes to say that this gap is factory installed. There are bound to be problems in anything we do. The people of Israel, for example, would encounter many obstacles as they went about conquering the remaining enemies in the Promised Land.

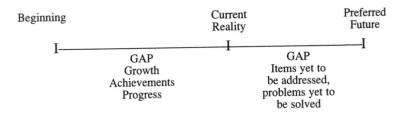

If we focus only on the gap of problems yet to be solved we become frustrated and discouraged. This gap can't be completely eliminated, but it can be balanced with another GAP—Growth, Achievements, Progress. This GAP represents the distance between where we began and our current situation—all that has been done by God's grace. I periodically list areas that have shown growth, achievements that have been made, and progress that has been evidenced. For the Israelites, the GAP included all the land that had been taken and the battles that God had won for them. They were no longer desert nomads; they were inhabitants of the land promised to them by God.

Some time ago a friend of mine was feeling overwhelmed by the leadership challenges that lay ahead. In conversation, he began to list them—programs to be improved, board members to be developed, facility changes to be made. He expressed doubts about his ability to lead from that point forward. Then the conversation shifted to the things he had accomplished. We talked about how he had helped the church relocate, built a new facility, brought improvements to the worship service, and upgraded the children's ministry. His doubts dissipated as he recalled what had been done.

In which gap do you tend to dwell? Do you visit the GAP of ground that has been gained and then ask God for a greater vision of what is yet to be done, even if you are not the one to do it? Or do you focus on what is yet to be done? Beware of the failure to count your blessings. Let past victories fuel your faith for the challenges still ahead.

How Will I Challenge Others

How will I challenge others to fully obey? Joshua discovered the personal benefits of fully obeying God. He was not a perfect leader—God's Word itself records some of his failures, as it does the failures of many spiritual leaders. But he had been largely successful in responding to God's command: "Be strong and very courageous. Be careful to obey all the law my servant Moses gave you; do not turn from it to the right or to the left, that you may be successful wherever you go" (Josh. 1:7). We hear the ring of that challenge in Joshua's final words to the people of Israel—"Be very strong; be very careful to obey all that is written in the Book of the Law of Moses, without turning aside to the right or to the left" (Josh. 23:6).

Joshua was explicit about what disobedience ("turning aside to the right or to the left") would look like for them. He named the sins to which they would be most susceptible. He warned against associating with the nations that remained in the Promised Land. He forbade the worshiping or serving of their gods, or even the mention of their names in making an oath. He banned alliances and intermarriage with other nations so that the Israelites would remain purely and fully dependent upon their God (Josh. 23:7, 12).

Joshua made it clear that in order to obey, the Israelites must "hold fast to the Lord [their] God" (Josh. 23:8). What does it mean to "hold fast," to not "turn aside to the right or the left"? As I've sought to live my life in complete devotion to God, I've identified two factors that contribute to full obedience, and for each factor, two forms of subtle disobedience that undermine it.

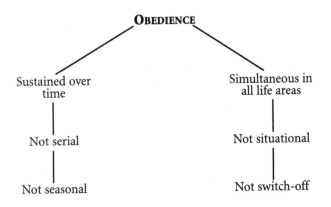

Obedience Factor One: Sustainability. Am I able to obey God fully, not in this moment only but for several hours in a row? Several days or weeks in a row? Several months or years in a row? How long can I sustain my attitude of complete surrender to Him? The more often I act in obedience, the more firmly ingrained the habits of obedience become in me.

One form of subtle disobedience that undermines sustained obedience is what I call *serial obedience.* This is especially dangerous because it *looks* like complete obedience. I borrowed the concept from Christian pollster George Barna, who identified the cultural trend called *serial monogamy*—being fully devoted to one spouse at a time as opposed to one spouse for a lifetime. Serial obedience is obeying God in one area of life at a time, then moving on to another area of obedience.

I observe this pattern whenever our teaching team presents a series of messages. For instance, we recently communicated God's truth about money. Many people were motivated to obey God in the area of finances as a result of that series. Then the team taught a series on biblical truths for relationships. Again many people responded, this time making the commitment to obey God in their relationships. The problem was that they dropped their commitment to obedience in finances, replacing it with a commitment to obedience in relationships. But genuine obedience is built layer upon layer, so that obedience in each area is sustained over time. Obedience in one area is added atop obedience in another, building a multi-layered foundation of full obedience to God.

A second form of subtle disobedience is *seasonal obedience.* Seasonal obedience is being obedient for certain seasons of life but excusing disobedience at other times. It's a high school or college student excusing moral compromises, claiming she'll get serious about Christian character after she finishes school. It's a young married couple failing to connect with a Christian community through a church or small group because they don't want to be "tied down," saying that they'll make that commitment when they have children. It's a retired person excusing his unwillingness to contribute time and money by claiming he's given enough already and that it's time for younger people to take over.

Sustained obedience is a commitment to honor God in every season of life, from the moment of new birth until the moment of appearing in God's presence.

Obedience Factor Two: Simultaneity. Can I obey God fully, not just in one area, but in many areas at the same time? In the words of 1 Pet. 1:15—"But just as he who called you is holy, so be holy in all you do." Holy in all we do. Holy in all areas of life. This is obedience in every dimension of my personal life—how I manage my physical desires, the thoughts I entertain, the feelings I nurture, the choices I make. It is comprehensive commitment, full surrender.

Simultaneous obedience is subtly undermined by *situational obedience.* Situational obedience is obedience that is dependent upon current circumstances. I may be a fully devoted disciple at church or at home but less devoted at my work or in school. I may be spiritually disciplined when I'm in town but make spiritual compromises when business travel takes me out of town. I may praise God openly with one group of friends but conveniently fail to mention my Christian faith when I'm with another group of people.

Another form of subtle disobedience that undermines simultaneous obedience is what I call *switch-off obedience.* This is a spiritual form of the game Let's Make a Deal. Switch-off obedience is when we negotiate with God rather than obeying Him fully. It is promising to devote extra money to God so we don't have to give any time, or vice versa. It's promising to live by His standards in relationships while compromising His standards for physical well-being through gluttony or sloth. It is diverting our attention away from God's conviction in one area by concentrating on our obedience in another.

Sustained, simultaneous obedience is the relentless pursuit of holiness in all of the places and times of my life. It is nothing short of full surrender. Anything less will result in devastating consequences. For the people of Israel, disobedience would have meant the withdrawal of God's support and their certain defeat (Josh. 23:13, 15–16).

RESOURCES

A fourth leadership question prompted by Joshua's farewell speech is this: What is the greatest resource for significant living? There are many resources that enrich the life of a leader. Educational opportunities can greatly enhance one's skills. Financial resources can provide experiences that refine or refresh. Good relationships are a resource that grants access to the wisdom and support of others. Acknowledging these resources not only increases our gratitude but also raises our awareness of how they might be managed effectively.

Joshua's farewell speech included a reminder of Israel's greatest resource—God, who fought for them (Josh. 23:9–11). Because He was on their side, no one had been able to withstand them. A single

Israelite had the ability to rout a thousand of the enemy. We gain tremendous energy from joining God in something He has decided to do. No other resource can compare to His power.

In the Old Testament the bestowal of God's power and presence was often call an *anointing*. It was the recognition that God had empowered a particular person for a particular task. That anointing could have been given for religious service, as in the case of a prophet or a priest. Or it might have been given for national service, as in the case of a king. When the favor of God rested upon a person, no human obstacle or liability could stand in the way.

It's been my privilege to be part of such a movement of God. There is nothing more humbling than to recognize that God is doing things through you that you could never have imagined doing on your own—and that He could just as easily have accomplished through someone else.

Joshua experienced this anointing, and the leaders around him shared in it. This resource, Joshua advised, would continue to be available for as long as they loved the Lord their God (Josh. 23:11). To love God completely is the fulfillment of the greatest commandment and the doorway to a life anointed by God.

PROMISES

Joshua's speech prompts me to ask a fifth question about the latter part of my leadership: What are the promises to be kept? Joshua reminded Israel's leaders of their covenant with God. A covenant is a contract, a record of commitments that have been made by two parties. In the Old Testament, some covenants were made between two people, others between two nations. The covenant Joshua recalled was a covenant between God and His people. The God of Israel was a covenant-making and covenant-keeping God.

Most covenants contained a historical prologue—a record of the events leading up to the making of the covenant. In his farewell speech, Joshua recounted the historical prologue to Israel's covenant with God (Josh. 24:1–13). This brief history provided the context for God's present work. Hearing a bit of history reminds us that we only have one place in time; God's plan preceded us and will continue after us. Taking possession of the Promised Land fulfilled a covenant that God first made with Abraham and then with Moses. The people of Israel were reminded that it was their turn to live up to the promises of the ancient covenant, fully confident that God would always live up to His part of the bargain.

So Joshua called the people to make a decision: "Choose for yourselves this day whom you will serve" (Josh. 24:14–15). It was necessary for each generation to affirm its commitment to abide by the covenant. Joshua reminded them that the choice was theirs. They could affirm their covenant with the Lord, serving Him with all faithfulness. Or they could make a covenant with other gods, like those served by their ancestors or those worshiped by the inhabitants of Canaan.

Joshua indicated his own choice in perhaps the most quoted verse in the book of Joshua—"But as for me and my household, we will serve the LORD" (24:15). Like any good leader, he invited the people to follow his example. The Apostle Paul did much the same when he invited others to, "Follow me as I follow Christ." A leader incarnates full devotion to God.

The people respond to Joshua by affirming their desire to obey the Lord their God (Josh. 24:16–18). They recognized that it was God who had delivered and protected them in the past. He had been their God and would continue to be.

Joshua's response to their affirmation is not what I would have expected. Rather than cheering them on, he flatly stated that they were unable to do what they said. They would not keep their promises to God, Joshua predicted, and there would be consequences for the inevitable break of their allegiance to Him (Josh. 24:19–20). That was hardly a motivational speech! Yet the people repeated their choice, agreeing to throw away their false gods and yield their hearts fully to the Lord. They witnessed their choice by erecting a stone monument (Josh. 24:22–27). The goal, you see, was not outward conformity to the stipulations of the covenant. The goal was nothing less than the complete devotion of their hearts to God.

Why did Joshua focus the challenge of his farewell address on the people's covenant with God? Because the covenant was a vivid reminder that life is not, ultimately, about the relationship between people and their leader. It is about the relationship between people and their God. Good spiritual leaders faithfully shepherd their people and develop close bonds with them. Yet they constantly remind them that their primary allegiance is to God, not the leader. Leaders come and go. God is the same yesterday, today, and forever. Only He can give lasting significance to life.

WHAT SUMMARIZES MY LIFE

What statement will summarize my life and ministry? Once the people had confirmed their covenant choice (Josh. 24:21–22), Joshua sent them away. Soon after that, Joshua passed away. Scripture records this epitaph for Israel's great leader: Servant of the LORD. What an affirmation! Just as Moses before him had been called as the Lord's servant, so Joshua received this honored description. Short but eternally significant, that may be the best memorial a spiritual leader could hope for.

My accountability partner has a custom license plate on his car. The message consists of five letters—TKASG. Those letters represent his life's mission "to know and serve God." He is a devoted husband and father, a successful businessman, and one who consistently orders his life around eternal priorities. Yet he uses that simple phrase to maintain his focus on the real bottom line, knowing and serving God.

What statement will best describe your life and ministry? When I think about that question, I try to imagine the answer from God's perspective because it's His "well done, good and faithful servant" that I'm living for. Whatever statement you choose to live by, it should be a statement that captures both your character and your calling.

For several years I've used a self-assessment tool called a *life arrow*. This process, using the shaft of an arrow as a model, helps me to identify the people who have shaped me, the opportunities that have stretched me, the resources that have supported me, and the problems that have refined me. The tip of the arrow is a brief statement of what I hope these forces in my life will lead to. That summary statement helps me focus on the legacy I hope to leave rather than the obstacles encountered along the way.

WHO WILL COME NEXT

The last question for leaders prompted by Joshua's farewell speech is based on something he *didn't* say: Who are the leaders who will come next? If Moses passed the baton of leadership to Joshua, to whom did Joshua pass it? Did Joshua fail to make a transfer of power? Did he opt for leadership by committee (the "elders who outlived him" are referred to in Josh. 24:31)? Did Joshua think that having the land would be a substitute for having a leader?

There is no lasting success without successors. The passing of a long-term leader often results in a leadership vacuum. That can usually be avoided by careful succession planning. The first step in a succession plan may be to determine what form of leadership will be appropriate for the next stage in a movement of God. Perhaps Joshua sensed that decentralized leadership would be needed to settle the Promised Land. God often uses a dynamic person early in the development of an initiative, then uses a team of people to manage the results of that venture.

The second step in a succession plan is to define the process by which the new leader or leaders will be selected. I have assisted our church board in developing a succession plan to be used for selecting the leader or leaders who will come after me. Because I have served as senior pastor for over two decades, very few of our members have witnessed a succession in that role. By constitution, I will not select the leader who follows me. Yet I do want the process to be clearly understood so that definite steps can be taken at that critical juncture.

Parts of the plan were a bit unsettling to write. What would happen if I were to fail morally? What would happen if I didn't think it was time for me to leave but the congregation did? Thinking through various negative scenarios strengthened my resolve to ensure that they never come true! The plan specifies what actions are to be taken, where the authority would rest, and whom should be consulted in each case. The plan is reviewed on an annual basis by our board and is available to the congregation. Knowing that the possibility of succession has been considered and planned for has provided a sense of assurance for our leaders.

It's my habit to follow a daily schedule for Bible reading so that I read the entire Bible in one year. The last time I read the books of Kings and Chronicles, I was disheartened to read of all the kings who started well but didn't finish well. The Living Bible describes a few of them this way:

Uzziah. "So he became famous, for the Lord helped him wonderfully until he was very powerful. But at that point he became proud—and corrupt" (2 Chron. 26:15–16).

Joash. "Joash tried hard to please the Lord all during the lifetime of Jehoida the priest . . . But after his death the leaders of Judah came to King Joash and induced him to abandon the Temple of the God of their ancestors, and to worship shame-idols instead!" (2 Chron. 24:2, 17).

Jehoshaphat. "But at the close of his life, Jehoshaphat, king of Judah, went into partnership with Ahaziah, king of Israel, who was a very wicked man" (2 Chron. 20:36).

Reading about these men reminds me that spiritual leaders are never beyond temptation. I recall the wise words of one pastor I know whose son asked him to promise that he would never fall morally. The pastor responded, "Son, I can never guarantee that I will not fall. I can only assure you that I'll start every day on my knees, humbly asking God to give me the strength and grace I need to obey Him in that day. I'll do that day after day until I draw my last breath." A daily affirmation of obedience leads to a lifetime of faithfulness.

I sometimes say to members of our staff, "Let's live our lives fully for the Lord. Someday we'll sit on a porch in our rocking chairs, sipping lemonade, and recall what a joy it has been to serve God our whole lives. We'll talk about the victories won and the lessons learned." There could be nothing simpler and sweeter.

Recently I attended a creative arts conference with nine of our staff and lay musicians, dancers, dramatists, and visual artists. I had the privilege of praying for them as the conference drew to a close. As the ten of us joined hands, I asked that God would protect us. That all of us would honor Him all of our lives. And that someday, on some earthly or heavenly porch, we'd be able to share the joy of having served Him until we went to be with Him.

That's my prayer for you as well.

PERSONAL REFLECTION

1. Read John 17:4. What do you see as the work God has given you to do? How will you know when it is completed?

2. Who are people you trust to give you honest feedback?

3. What are the most significant blessings in your personal life?

4. In what areas do you struggle most to be obedient?

5. What long-term promises have you made (for example, wedding vows or pledges made when dedicating children)?

6. What short-term promises have you made (such as a commitment to a small group or membership in a recreational league)?

Inventory for Spiritual Leaders

1. What blessings do you count as most significant in your ministry?

2. As you look to the future, what work do you see that is yet to be done?

3. GAP management exercise.

Beginning	Current Reality	Preferred Future
I———————————	—I———————	——————I

Areas of Growth, Achievement, Progress: Items Yet to Be Addressed:

_____   _____

_____   _____

_____   _____

_____   _____

4. With what resources has God blessed you?

   Educational

   Financial

   Relational

   Spiritual

   Other

5. Do you have a succession plan for your ministry?

6. As a concluding exercise, write your ideal farewell speech. How must you live and lead from this day forward if that speech is to truly depict your legacy?

Joshua's Journal

Lord, the final word on my life will not be mine, but Yours. I want to so live that someday I will hear Your "well done." I may not be able to fully envision what my contribution is to be, yet I ask that You would give me glimpses of it, and I promise to act upon what You show me. Help me to live with an open heart and an open hand, recognizing that Your eternal work did not begin with me and will not end with me. I realize that's the only way I can live freely and lead fully. Amen.

APPENDIX A

—⁓—

1. ACCOUNTABILITY

We believe in the need to hold each other accountable. This is evidenced by living a life of integrity according to biblical principles. Since God loves us the way we are but expects growth from us, accountability involves challenging, encouraging, and building each other up in His redemptive grace.

Prov. 27:17; Eccles. 4:9–12; Matt. 18:15–20; Gal. 6:1–5; 1 Thess. 5:11; Heb. 10:24–25; 13:17; James 5:16.

Value Ventures

_____ I have an accountability partnership to reinforce specific spiritual commitments.

_____ I am responsive to spiritual authority and a supportive follower of my leaders.

_____ I regularly encourage others in their faith and have identified specific people to consistently encourage.

_____ When I experience conflict in relationships, I follow a biblical conflict resolution process.

_____ I am teachable and humbly receive the perspectives of others.

Value Vampires

____ There are many parts of my life completely unknown by others.

____ I tend to be very individualistic with a "lone-ranger, do-it-your-self" approach to Christianity.

____ I tend to distrust others and devalue relationships that are "uncomfortably close" spiritually.

____ My previous negative experiences with authority contribute to detachment or rebellion.

2. AWARENESS OF AND BIBLICAL APPROACH TO CULTURAL ISSUES

We believe that we need to be aware of those cultural issues that impact the community and God's Church and yet not be corrupted by worldly values. Our actions and responses must be based on biblical truth, God's redemptive grace, and our desire to reach out to those needing the healing love of Jesus Christ.

1 Chron. 12:32; Matt. 5:13–16; Mark 8:34–38; Luke 5:38; Acts 17:22–23; Rom. 12:2; 1 Cor. 9:22; 2 Cor. 6:14–7:1; 10:1–5; Eph. 5:15–16; 1 Tim. 6:6–10; 1 Pet. 3:15; 1 John 2:15–17

Value Ventures

____ I read and learn about cultural trends affecting Christianity.

____ I have identified and consider the thoughts of modern-day prophets (i.e. Chuck Colson, Keith Drury, etc.)

____ I am part of a partnership or group that makes me aware of spiritual "drift" in my life, or areas in my life shaped more by the culture than by Christ.

Value Vampires

____ My tendency is to respond to a new idea because "everyone is doing it."

____ My desire to fit in or be "successful" pulls me away from biblical values.

3. BIBLICAL COMMUNICATION

We believe that the Bible, God's inspired Word, is our foundation and is to be consistently communicated by such forms as teaching, preaching, correcting, rebuking, witnessing, and the creative arts. The biblical pattern of communication is to speak the truth in love, therefore negative forms of communication such as non-constructive criticism, gossip, and slander are not biblical, are unacceptable, and will be properly addressed.

Ps. 119:11, 105; Acts 2:42; Rom. 12:6–7; Eph. 4:15; 6:19–20; Col. 3:16; 1 Tim. 3:2; 5:17; 2 Tim. 2:16; 3:16–17: Heb. 4:12; James 1:22; 1 Pet. 3:15; 4:10; 2 John 1:10–11

Value Ventures

____ I try to sense what will build a person up spiritually before I speak.

____ I guard my tongue, filtering my thoughts with God's Word before I speak.

____ I am eager to receive God's Word through a variety of communication channels.

Values Vampires

____ I tend to distort the truth through exaggeration, deception, misrepresentation, etc.

____ My communication is shaped more by family history or personal patterns than by God's Word.

____ I am biblically illiterate, which means I'm ill-equipped to share biblical truth with others.

____ I am unwilling to communicate at times, withdrawing rather than responding to God's prompting to "speak the truth in love."

4. FELLOWSHIP

We believe that God created us to be in fellowship with one another. In a large church, we as a congregation must be intentional about cultivating relationships. Fellowship opportunities where deepening relationships can be developed are found in a variety of focused ministries and smaller group settings.

Acts 2:42–47; 4:32–35; Rom. 12:5; Phil. 2:1–4; 1 Pet. 4:9; 1 John 1:7

Value Ventures

____ I am fully engaged in a small group, serving team, or Adult Bible Connection (ABC).

____ I have a commitment to meet a new person at KCC regularly.

____ After services or events, I generally hang around a bit to talk with others.

____ While talking with established friends, I also seek to include newer people in our conversations.

Value Vampires

____ I associate only with those that I have a lot in common with socially, ethnically, generationally, or economically.

____ I wait for others to take the initiative in beginning a conversation or forming a relationship.

____ I have lots of acquaintances, but no close friends.

____ My conversations with other Christians could rarely be characterized as "spiritual"—they cover only superficial topics.

5. GROWING RELATIONSHIP WITH JESUS CHRIST DEMONSTRATED BY LIFE CHANGE

We believe that a Christian life begins when we confess our sins, accept Christ as our personal Savior, and commit to following Him.

The Holy Spirit indwells our lives, empowering us for obedience and transforming us to be more Christlike. To be vibrant, this relationship must be growing and we must demonstrate that Jesus Christ is Lord of our life.

Matt. 22:37; John 15:1–2, 5–8, 10; Rom. 6:1–4, 11–18; 12:1–2; 2 Cor. 5:17; Gal. 5:16–26; Eph. 4:15, 20–24; Col. 2:6–7; 1 John 2:6; 5:2–3.

Value Ventures

____ I pray regularly, seeking to listen to what God's Spirit may say to me about areas in my life where I need growth or change.

____ I can identify areas in my spiritual walk where I've grown recently.

____ My character is bearing more of the fruit of the Spirit.

____ I repent when God convicts me, rather than harboring unresolved sin.

Value Vampires

____ I've been on a spiritual plateau for some time, having settled into a comfort zone.

____ I make trade-offs, growing in some aspects of faith but not in others

____ I use "grace" as an excuse for sin rather than as a source of power for holy living.

____ I'm drifting backward, but am indecisive about steps forward in faith.

6. LOVING ONE ANOTHER

We believe that Jesus commanded us to love our neighbors and enemies. Jesus demonstrated an attitude of love and acceptance for us to follow. Love is an unselfish concern that freely accepts another and seeks God's best for them.

Lev. 19:18; Matt. 22:37–39; Luke 10:30–37; John 13:34–35; Rom. 13:9–10; 15:7; 1 Cor. 13; 1 John 3:14–18; 4:7–12.

Value Ventures

____ I am generous in meeting the needs of others.

____ I am a good listener, seeking to understand a person's needs so I can pray for them more specifically.

____ I am gracious to people even if I find it difficult to personally relate to them.

Value Vampires

____ I have allowed a root of bitterness over a past disappointment to poison relationships.

____ When others hurt me, I seek ways of getting vengeance.

____ I am critical of or condescending toward others, focusing on faults rather than strengths.

____ I am unforgiving and unwilling to follow the path of biblical resolution of conflicts.

7. PRAYER

We believe that God desires our prayers and God's house is to be a house of prayer. Jesus taught us how to pray and demonstrated the power of prayer. Prayer is a two-way communication with the Almighty God.

Matt. 5:44; 6:5–15; John 17; Eph. 6:18–20; Phil. 4:6–7; 1 Thess. 5:17; 1 Tim. 2:1–8;

Value Ventures

____ I consistently set aside time for personal prayer.

____ I participate in a prayer group or prayer time in a small group, ABC, or serving team.

____ I keep a list of people and needs to remember in prayer.

____ I value quiet times to listen in prayer to the "still, small voice of the Spirit."

____ If God prompts me I go forward during public service prayer times.

____ I am willing to pray for someone "on the spot" who needs my prayers.

Value Vampires

____ I offer mindless prayers, many times not even knowing what I've said in prayer.

____ I offer prayers just to impress others.

____ I say I'll pray for someone and then forget to do it.

8. REACHING OUT TO THE LOST

We believe that God has given us the responsibility to share the way of salvation through Jesus Christ with people headed to an eternity separated from God. Hell is a real place and real people go there. The Holy Spirit empowers us to reach these people whether across the street or around the world.

Matt. 5:13–16; 9:12, 37–38; 28:16–20; Acts 1:8; 2:42–47; 5:28–29, 32; 13:47; 1 Pet. 3:15.

Value Ventures

____ I have a prayer (Four Heaven's Sake) list of unchurched acquaintances and family.

____ I know my most natural evangelistic style and seek out ways to utilize it.

____ I can express my personal testimony and share it if the opportunity arises.

_____ I carry a tract or am prepared to make a verbal presentation of the gospel.

Value Vampires

_____ Almost all of my relationships are with other Christians.

_____ I'm uncomfortable with the idea of evangelism, I rationalize that "all paths lead to God," or "almost everyone goes to heaven," or "hell is not a real place."

_____ I stay in my comfort zone rather than courageously "pay the price of outreach" in time, money, inconvenience, possible rejection.

9. SERVANTHOOD THROUGH GIFT-BASED MINISTRY

We believe that God calls us to serve Him by serving others as modeled by Jesus' words and actions. We believe that God provides our church with all the spiritual gifts necessary to complete the work He has given us. It is our duty as Christians to discover those gifts and to use them to build each other up and reach out to our community.

Matt. 4:10; Mark 9:35; John 3:30; 13:5–17; Acts 6:2–4; Rom. 12:3–9; 1 Cor. 12:4–6; 15:58; Gal. 1:10; Eph. 4:11–12; Phil. 2:5–11; 1 Pet. 4:8–11

Value Ventures

_____ I have identified my ministry passions.

_____ I understand and use my spiritual gifts.

_____ I know my personality strengths and how I can build on them to serve.

_____ I regularly invest time and money to benefit others.

Value Vampires

_____ I'm a consumer, receiving more from others than I give to others.

____ I view myself as "retired" or "I've done my part"—"it's some-one else's turn."

____ I use "it's not my gift" as an excuse for not periodically serving in practical ways.

10. STEWARDSHIP

We believe that everything belongs to God. Being a good stew-ard means proper management of what God has given us and giving back to God what He desires. God holds us accountable for all He has entrusted to us.

Gen. 1:1, 26–28; 1 Chron. 29:11; Ps. 24:1; 89:8–13; Eccles. 5:19; Mal. 3:8–9; Matt. 6:21; Luke 19:12–26; John 3:27; Acts 20:35; Rom. 11:35; Eph. 4:28; Col. 1:15–17; 1 Tim. 6:17–19

Value Ventures

____ I regularly and prayerfully acknowledge that "God owns it all."

____ I ask God how He wants me to invest the money, time, and abil-ity He has entrusted to me.

____ I seek out opportunities to learn how to more effectively man-age the resources God has entrusted to me.

Value Vampires

____ I embezzle from God, consuming my material blessings and giving only the leftovers.

____ I allow excessive debt to rob me of financial freedom.

____ I give in to the lure of materialism, leading to indulgence rather than simplicity.

____ I fail to enjoy what God has entrusted to me.

11. WORSHIP

We believe that we were created to worship God the Father, Son, and Holy Spirit. We worship God as we come together in public services, in smaller settings, and in private devotional times. We worship God when we submit ourselves to Him. The focus of our worship is not ourselves but God.

> 1 Chron. 16:29; Ps. 29:1–2; 63:4–5; 95:1–8; 100:1–2; 135:1–3; Isa. 6:1–4; Luke 4:8; John 4:23–24; Acts 2:42–47; Rom. 1:20–23; 12:1; Eph. 5:19–20; Phil. 3:3; Heb. 10:25; Rev. 4:3–11; 7:9–12.

Value Ventures

____ I spend time alone in worship—reading God's Word, praying, listening to Christian music, meditating, etc.

____ I come prepared to enter into times of public worship.

____ I engage in all the dimensions of worship—celebration, reflection, repentance, etc.—regardless of personal preference.

____ I attend public worship almost weekly, making it a priority.

Value Vampires

____ I am a spectator and critic, evaluating how well the people up front are doing.

____ I leave a service asking "Did I like it?" rather than asking "What did I offer to God today?"

____ I limit my expressions of worship to only the comfortable and familiar rather than seeking what God desires of me most of all.

____ I demean forms of worship that I experience as less meaningful even if others experience them as significant.

Appendix B

The Mission and Vision of Kentwood Community Church

Mission

The mission of Kentwood Community Church is to obey Christ by:

- Reaching out to spiritually lost people and

- Raising up fully committed believers who love God completely and others unconditionally.

Vision

The vision of Kentwood Community Church is to be a biblically functioning community with Spirit-empowered leadership who relentlessly pursue our God-given dream.

We dream of a place known as the hub of our community, where the immediate and ultimate needs of all people are met in a loving, safe, and encouraging atmosphere. The people who gather here will reflect all the ages, races, economic situations, and educational levels represented in our region. Much of our ministry will happen offsite, where we live and work, as well as through strategic partnerships with other organizations. Our central location will offer park-like property and multi-use facilities to minister to the total person—spiritually, emotionally, physically, and socially—with twenty-four-hour, seven-day-a-week availability.

We dream of hundreds of people making profession of faith and being baptized annually as first steps toward full maturity in Christ. This will happen because every KCCer is sharing the good news of Jesus Christ by praying for specific unchurched people in their realm of influence and inviting them to events and services with appropriate evangelistic intensity. KCCers are reaching out in a way that is consistent with their God-given evangelistic style and are equipped to share a verbal presentation of the gospel.

We dream of every believer serving as part of the body of Christ and under the Lordship of Christ. *Where* we serve is shaped by our passions, *what* we do utilizes our spiritual gifts, and *how* we serve is influenced by our personal style. More than volunteers who give of something that belongs to them, we are ministers who serve recognizing that all we are and have belongs to God. We dream of every believer exercising stewardship of their time, talents, and money, permitting an uninterrupted flow of resources from God through believers to benefit His kingdom.

We dream of every person being warmly welcomed in larger groups settings and being deeply affirmed and accountable in smaller group settings so we experience intimacy with God and vitality in interpersonal relationships. While many of these settings are intentional, relational vibrancy will also occur spontaneously in hallways, classrooms, and gathering places conducive to creating community.

We dream of thousands of believers actively worshiping God with various expressions in a variety of public services and private settings. While allowing people to connect in a way that is relevant to them, we resist any tendency to seek our preferences over God's presence. We seek to prayerfully prompt heartfelt praise, regular and specific repentance, bold asking, full submission to God's Spirit, and the lifelong learning and obeying of God's truth.

We dream of being a sending church, deploying people to provide the core for development of new churches and helping people to hear God's call into vocational ministry and missions, creating a movement that starts locally and ripples globally. We will seek to be a resource center for other churches denominationally, regionally, and internationally.

We pursue this vision fully confident that God who gave us this dream will carry it to completion until the day of Christ Jesus (Phil. 1:6).

NOTES

—⟨⟨⟨—

CHAPTER ONE: SLOW BUT SURE

1. See Christian A. Schwarz, *Natural Church Development* (Carol Stream, Ill.: ChurchSmart Resources, 1996).

2. Ibid., 53.

3. John C. Maxwell, *The 21 Irrefutable Laws of Leadership* (Nashville, Tenn.: Thomas Nelson Publishers, 1998), 1.

4. Wayne Schmidt and Yvonne Prowant, *Accountability: Becoming People of Integrity* (Indianapolis, Ind.: Wesley Press, 1991).

5. Bill Hybels and Mark Mittelberg, *Becoming a Contagious Christian* (Grand Rapids, Mich.: Zondervan Publishing House, 1994).

6. Jim Collins, *Good to Great* (New York: HarperCollins Publishers, 2001), 41.

7. Wayne Schmidt, *Leading When God Is Moving* (Indianapolis, Ind.: Wesley Press, 1996), 108–109.

CHAPTER TWO: CLARIFYING CORE COMMITMENTS

1. Daniel Goleman, *Emotional Intelligence: Why It Can Matter More Than IQ,* reprint ed. (New York: Bantam Books, 1997).

CHAPTER THREE: GOD'S POWER FOR GOD'S PURPOSE

1. Richard A. Swenson, *Margin* (Colorado Springs, Colo.: NavPress Publishing Group, 1992).

CHAPTER FOUR: OVERCOMING OBSTACLES

1. Dan Sullivan, "Seven Laws of Lifelong Growth," The Strategic

Coach, Inc. web site, October 2002: www.strategiccoach.com.

Chapter Five: The Debilitating Danger of Deception

1. Jim Collins, *Good to Great* (New York: HarperCollins Publishers, 2001), 126.

2. "The Emerging Role of the Executive Pastor," *Defining Moments* audio tape series (South Barrington, Ill.: Willow Creek Association, 2002).

Chapter Six: Maintaining Momentum

1. Robert Hanashiro, "Scandals nothing new to business guru," *USA Today*, 5 July 2002.

2. Richard Zalack, *Are You Doing Business or Building One?* (Brunswick, Ohio: Praxis Press, 2000), 30.

3. Warren Bennis and David Heenan, *Co-Leaders: The Power of Great Partnerships* (New York: John Wiley and Sons, Inc. 1999).

4. Zalack, *Doing Business,* 15.

Chapter Seven: The Crucible of Conflict

1. Larry L. McSwain, William C. Treadwell Jr., *Conflict Ministry in the Church* (Nashville, Tenn.: Broadman and Holman Publishers, 1981), 36.

2. Ibid., 42.

Chapter Eight: A Leader's Legacy

1. Stephen R. Covey, *The Seven Habits of Highly Effective People* (New York: Simon and Schuster, 1989), 98.

2. Richard G. Zalack, *Are You Doing Business or Building One?* (Brunswick, Ohio: Praxis Press, 2000), 8–9.